TIME

HORSES TO FOLLOW

2016/17 JUMPS SEASON

CONTENTS

TIMEF⌐RM

ISBN 978-0-9933900-4-3   Price £9.95

Printed and bound by
Charlesworth Press,
Wakefield, UK 01924 204830

SECTION

Timeform's Fifty To Follow, carefully chosen by members of Timeform's editorial staff, are listed below with their respective page numbers. A selection of ten (**marked in bold with a** ★) is made for those who prefer a smaller list.

The form summary for each horse is shown after its age, colour, sex and pedigree. The summary shows the distance, the state of the going and where the horse finished in each of its races since the start of the 2015/16 season. Performances are in chronological sequence with the date of its last race shown at the end (F–ran on Flat).

The distance of each race is given in furlongs. Steeplechase form figures are prefixed by the letter 'c', hurdle form figures by the letter 'h' and NH Flat race or bumper form figures by the letter 'b'.

The going is symbolised as follows: f–firm, m–good to firm; g–good, d–good to soft; s–soft; v–heavy.

Placings are indicated, up to the sixth place, by use of superior figures, an asterisk being used to denote a win and superior letters are used to convey what happened to a horse during the race: F–fell, pu–pulled up, ur–unseated rider, bd–brought down, su–slipped up, ro–ran out.

The Timeform Rating of a horse is simply the merit of the horse expressed in pounds and is arrived at by careful examination of its running against other horses. The ratings range from 175+ for the champions down to a figure of around 55 for selling platers. Symbols attached to the ratings: 'p'–likely to improve; 'P'–capable of much better form; '+'–the horse may be better than we have rated it.

Aloomomo (Fr)   h130 c138p

6 b.g. Tirwanako (Fr) – Kayola (Fr) (Royal Charter (Fr))
2015/16 c20s* c20d* c22.4s* h19.3s³ c20.4g⁶ Mar 15

Many may look at Aloomomo's profile and think he did all his improving last season, when he won handicap chases on his first three starts and improved almost two stone on Timeform ratings. That was his first full campaign with the excellent Warren Greatrex yard, however, and after shaping well at the Cheltenham Festival on his final outing, there must be a good chance the six-year-old can progress again in the new term.

The Greatrex stable evidently learned plenty about the ex-French Aloomomo when he made two winless starts for it at the back-end of 2014/15, as he came back with a bang when winning a two-and-a-half-mile handicap at Uttoxeter in late-October by twelve lengths. Aloomomo jumped superbly as he justified strong market support that day, and he did the same when winning twice in November, at Warwick and Newbury. Aloomomo was stepped back up in trip for the last-named race and beat his fifteen rivals by nine lengths and upwards, shrugging off a 14 lb higher mark in the process. Aloomomo then had a break before having his warm-up race for the Cheltenham Festival back over hurdles in February, finishing third of five to Yala Enki at Ascot. Aloomomo was again very well backed (3/1f) for the novices' handicap chase at the Festival and, while he could finish only sixth of twenty to Ballyalton, he went with enthusiasm for a long way before faltering on the run-in. Greatrex later explained: "Aloomomo ran well in ground that was too quick for him [at Cheltenham]. He travelled very well until the top of the hill but due to the ground, never finished as we would have hoped. We will look at races such as the Hennessy in the early part of the [new] season as possibles. I am still confident he has huge potential." We agree that Aloomomo remains a horse to follow, though whether the Hennessy Gold Cup is the right race for him remains to be seen—he's a strong-travelling prominent racer who is yet to prove himself beyond two and three-quarter miles and perhaps the big handicaps at around two and a half miles at Cheltenham (including the BetVictor Gold Cup, which was formerly the Paddy Power) are more suitable. **Warren Greatrex**

Conclusion: *Progressive in first full season with the Greatrex stable when winning three handicap chases in 2015/16 and should have even more to offer this term; reportedly being considered for the Hennessy, though the big Cheltenham handicaps at around 2½m could be more suitable*

Aqua Dude (Ire)   h142p

6 br.g. Flemensfirth (USA) – Miss Cozzene (Fr) (Solid Illusion (USA))
2015/16 h15.7s* h15.7d³ h15.7d^ur h20.3s* Mar 29

The 2016 Grand National will be remembered as the first renewal won by a novice since Mr What's success in 1958, with Rule The World also the first horse to lose his maiden status over fences in the world's greatest steeplechase since Voluptuary in 1884. Another feature of the latest Grand National was the big run of the 100/1-shot Vics Canvas who at thirteen became the oldest frame-finisher in the race this century. Finishing in the first four in the Grand National became something of a habit for owners William and Angela Rucker for several years as their State of Play (2009, 2010 and 2011) Cappa Bleu (2012 and 2013) and Alvarado (2014 and 2015; he missed the cut for the 2016 race before taking second in the Scottish version a week later) all achieved the feat, and it would be no surprise if the owners saw Aqua Dude as their next 'National' horse. Useful hurdler Aqua Dude has to prove he can jump fences first, but there are good reasons to think he can develop into a smart novice chaser in the new season.

Bought for €150,000 a week after easily winning his sole start in Irish points in April 2014, Aqua Dude made his first start under Rules in an Ascot bumper the following February, finishing only ninth of ten. Aqua Dude was given plenty more time before his hurdling debut last November, but it worked as he landed a novice event at Southwell by an easy two and a half lengths from subsequent winner Kerispers. Aqua Dude was rather unlucky on his next two starts, first when unsuited by a tactical race in a Grade 2 novice back at Ascot won by Yanworth, and then especially so when stumbling and unseating at the last when in front in a novice at Southwell. Aqua Dude made amends stepped up to two and a half miles at the latter track in March, a performance that probably set the tone for his future, with that trip now likely to prove a bare minimum for him. Aqua Dude looks on a fair BHA hurdles mark of 136 if connections do choose to remain over timber for the time being, but he's a well-made point winner by the sire of such as Imperial Commander and Tidal Bay and his future surely lies over fences. *Evan Williams*

Conclusion: *Showed very useful form as a novice hurdler in 2015/16 and remains fairly treated over timber off 136, but looks the sort to come into his own over fences; stays 2½m well*

Arpege d'Alene (Fr)   h148 c134+
6 gr.g. Dom Alco (Fr) – Joliette d'Alene (Fr) (Garde Royale)
2015/16 c20.2s² c23.4vᵖᵘ h23.6s* h24g² h24.7s Apr 9

Marcel Rolland has enjoyed plenty of success in France, including with the French Champion Hurdle winner Questarabad who was being talked about as a contender for the 2010 World Hurdle but never made the race. However, Rolland will surely have had one eye on British racing in recent seasons as he used to train, among others, Arpege d'Alene who made a winning hurdling debut/first start for his current connections at Ascot in November 2014 and won another race there (beat Tea For Two) from just two subsequent starts that term. Arpege d'Alene was sent off at 13/8f and 2/1 for his two outings over fences at the start of 2015/16, which wasn't a surprise given his profile, tall physique and the fact he's a half-brother to Hennessy winner Triolo d'Alene, but he was found to have suffered a breathing problem after his second to Junction Fourteen in a Grade 2 on his return and was then pulled up wearing a first-time tongue tie. With his chasing career on hold, and following a ten-week break, Arpege d'Alene bounced back to win a seventeen-runner handicap hurdle at Chepstow (again wearing a tongue strap) in February, rallying well after making a mess of the last to beat Dan Emmett by half a length. Arpege d'Alene improved again when beating all bar Mall Dini in the twenty-four runner Pertemps Final at the Cheltenham Festival three weeks later, and he shaped as if still in good form (with cheekpieces back on for the first time since his sole start in France) when mid-field in the nineteen-runner Grade 3 handicap won by Ubak at Aintree's Grand National meeting.

Connections have several options for Arpege d'Alene this season—which adds to his appeal—including returning to fences given he remains a novice in that sphere. A "lovely, big scopey horse" according to his trainer Paul Nicholls, who's sure to have given him some intensive schooling over the summer, Arpege d'Alene should pay his way this season. **Paul Nicholls**

Conclusion: *Won a big-field handicap hurdle (3m) last term and proved he doesn't need the mud when second in Pertemps Final; still feasibly-treated over timber, though does have the option of returning to fences as a novice (half-brother to Triolo d'Alene)*

Ballyoptic (Ire) ★   h146p

6 b.g. Old Vic – Lambourne Lace (Ire) (Un Desperado (Fr))
2015/16 b16v⁵ h20v* h19.9s* h24.7d* Apr 8

While recent winners of the Sefton Novices' Hurdle at Aintree have proved a rather mixed bag in terms of how their careers have progressed—or haven't—the 2015 renewal did go to last season's World Hurdle hero Thistlecrack, and it's envisaged that Ballyoptic will prove another good winner. After finding himself in front a fair way from home in the Sefton, Ballyoptic looked as if he would have to settle for a place when he was headed before two out by the favourite Bellshill, but that rival blundered at that flight and was then outbattled on the run-in by Ballyoptic who himself had hardly been foot-perfect over the final hurdle. The form would be franked when the runner-up won the equivalent race at the Punchestown Festival.

Ballyoptic is the latest in a long line of notable horses originally owned by Wilson Dennison in Irish points; Bellshill is actually among them too, as are Briar Hill, Shaneshill and Yorkhill. Ballyoptic raced five times for trainer Ian Ferguson in that sphere, winning once and finishing placed three times, and then made his debut under Rules for the same handler in a Down Royal bumper on Boxing Day, finishing fifth of sixteen. Ballyoptic was then presumably bought privately by his current connections, and he made his winning hurdling debut on heavy ground at Ffos Las in February, before following up on soft going at Uttoxeter in March. Ballyoptic dispelled any notion that he might simply be a mudlark in winning the Sefton, when the step up to three miles was undoubtedly a catalyst for further improvement. "Chasing is his future, but let's look at long-distance hurdles next season to start off with," said Ballyoptic's trainer Nigel Twiston-Davies after Aintree, which suggests races like the Long Walk Hurdle, Long Distance Hurdle, Cleeve Hurdle and World Hurdle (all won by Thistlecrack last season) could feature on his agenda this term. The well-made Ballyoptic also looks the type to make a chaser should his connections have a change of heart. **Nigel Twiston-Davies**

Conclusion: *Made rapid progress over hurdles last term, with his three wins including the Sefton Novices' at Aintree; live World Hurdle candidate, especially as Thistlecrack goes chasing, though also looks the type to make a chaser himself— either way he'll win more good races*

Dan Barber, Jumps Editor (Ballyoptic): *"Nigel Twiston-Davies has a lot of horses in his yard with wide-ranging abilities, however he knows a good one when he sees one, as the exploits of Bindaree, Imperial Commander, and The New One will attest to. The new 'B-Brigade', consisting of Blaklion, Ballyandy and Ballyoptic, look set to provide Twiston-Davies with a profitable season, and the last-named could rise to the top. Winner of the Sefton Novices' at Aintree, Ballyoptic could follow the same path trodden by the previous year's winner Thistlecrack, and he looks capable of dominating a staying division which looks wide-open following Thistlecrack's switch to chasing."*

Bekkensfirth   h108 c134p

7 b.g. Flemensfirth (USA) – Bekkaria (Fr) (Clafouti (Fr))
2015/16 h16g³ h19.3g c20.2v* c20.5d² Dec 26

At this stage last year Bekkensfirth had already returned over hurdles without success, but it was when switched to chasing in December that he really clicked into gear, perhaps unsurprisingly given he's a half-brother to French chase winners Nemenchka and Beni Abbes. Bekkensfirth had been given an opening mark of 115 over hurdles and could do no better than ninth of fifteen in an Ascot handicap on his second start back last October, but he took a big leap forward (having been dropped only 3 lb) when making a successful chasing debut in a Leicester novices' handicap (heavy going) six weeks later by thirteen lengths from ten rivals, in the process proving that it certainly wasn't the step up to two and a half miles that had beaten him the time before. The handicapper presumably crossed Dan Skelton firmly off his Christmas card list as he handed out a 10 lb rise to Bekkensfirth, but it was less the new mark that beat him on his next start—when a three-quarter-length second to Full Shift (pair clear) in a novices' handicap at Kempton on Boxing Day—and more the bad mistake he made three out. Bekkensfirth's jumping had again been good otherwise. With just seven runs under his belt, Bekkensfirth is lightly raced for his age and looks open to more improvement over fences; he should win another handicap or two in 2017 (he won't return until after Christmas according to his trainer). **Dan Skelton**

Conclusion: *Took well to chasing in two starts over the larger obstacles last term and should have more to offer when he returns; stays 2½m and acts on heavy going, but doesn't need the mud*

Bennys King (Ire) h118p

5 b.g. Beneficial – Hellofafaithful (Ire) (Oscar (Ire))
2015/16 h15.3s^6 h16v^2 h16s^2 :: 2016/17 h19.6g^2 Apr 29

If we were to play a racing version of a word association game, whereby the first term which springs to mind when "Cheltenham" is mentioned is "Festival" then surely "Venetia Williams" would be quickly followed by "stayer". The Herefordshire-based trainer has long been known for her skill with horses who need further than two and a half miles, and we're confident she can work her magic with Bennys King.

Bennys King is certainly bred to need time and distance, by the sire of More of That out of a point-winning close relative of the very smart three-mile chaser Master of The Hall, and so it was to his credit that he was able to go so close (short-head second to Mere Anarchy) in a two-mile Chepstow novice on his third start over hurdles. Unsurprisingly, Bennys King improved again stepped up to two and a half miles in a similar race at Bangor on his next outing, again closing all the way to the line as he filled the runner-up spot for the third straight race behind the promising Newsworthy. Bennys King was still rough around the edges there and should progress well as his stamina is further drawn out in the new season. He's certainly in the right hands and is expected to win a staying handicap hurdle or two this term.
Venetia Williams

Conclusion: *Made steady progress in 2015/16 and should really come into his own when sent over further than 2½m this season; seems versatile regards ground and can win a handicap hurdle or two*

Betameche (Fr) ★ b119p

5 gr.g. Kapgarde (Fr) – Kaldona (Fr) (Kaldoun (Fr))
2015/16 b16.4v* b15.8s* Apr 1

The Tonight Show Starring Jimmy Fallon began a new challenge last year: the Quadruple Crown, which involved winning the Kentucky Derby, Preakness Stakes, Belmont Stakes and a mini-motorbike race against the host around the television studio. It was won at the first time of asking by Victor Espinoza who, fresh from completing the American Triple Crown aboard American Pharoah, won the final leg despite taking an early wrong turn. Fallon also had a panel of puppies try to predict the winner of the 2016 Kentucky Derby earlier this year—they were unsuccessful—and his (rather tenuous) link to horse racing will continue through Betameche, who takes his name from the 'irritating troll doll look-alike' voiced by Fallon in the 2006 children's film Arthur And The Invisibles.

Betameche was owned by Langdale Bloodstock and trained by Nicky Richards when he made a winning debut at Newcastle, but he'd been bought privately by Judy Craymer and sent to Dan Skelton before his next start in a similar race at Wetherby four months later. Betameche again scored by a clear margin, this time in the hands of the Skelton stable's 5-lb claimer Bridget Andrews, and the form looked strong with the first three all previous winners. In fact, Timeform ratings suggest Betameche's performance would have been good enough to see him fight out the placings in the Champion Bumper at Cheltenham. Betameche is a half-brother to four winners, including the useful hurdler/fairly useful chaser Bold Addition, who was trained by Paul Nicholls at the time when Skelton was his assistant. Betameche presumably gets his speed from his dam Kaldona, who won at around a mile and quarter on the Flat in France, and he's clearly one to look forward to in the new season. ***Dan Skelton***

Conclusion: *Unbeaten in two starts in bumpers, and looks an exciting prospect for novices hurdles; has plenty of speed though will probably stay further than 2m*

Blue Rambler   h122p

6 b.g. Monsun (Ger) – La Nuit Rose (Fr) (Rainbow Quest (USA))
2015/16 h15.7s³ h19.4s² h15.8s² h18.6s⁵ Sep 3 (F)

Some members of the *Fifty* announce themselves as possible inclusions at the earliest stage in the process. Others, like Blue Rambler, force their way in at the eleventh hour.

It was as recently as the first weekend in September that Blue Rambler made his compelling case, and it wasn't even in a jumps race. Sent off at 33/1 for the handicap formerly known as the Old Borough Cup at Haydock, making his debut for Ian Williams, Blue Rambler (like most of the runners) was up against it soon after the start when the eventual winner Intense Tango was gifted the easiest of leads. It was, therefore, some effort from Blue Rambler to claim third of seventeen, finishing strongly and looking all about stamina on just his second start over a staying trip on the Flat. That was a decidedly useful performance from Blue Rambler from a BHA mark of 99, and also one which suggests his new yard can place him to advantage back over hurdles in the coming months, with his form in a mere four-race spell as a novice for his former trainer John Ferguson having resulted in a potentially favourable official rating of 122. And as if a lenient mark wasn't enough, there is still the stamina angle to exploit with Blue Rambler—he's unraced at a full two and a half miles and beyond over jumps and, unlike many ex-Flat recruits, such trips on testing ground shouldn't hold any fears.

Better late than never, then. Or at least that's the hope with Blue Rambler! ***Ian Williams***

Conclusion: *Plenty to like about his staying-on third in a top Flat handicap in September on his stable debut and will look potentially well treated if returned to hurdling; should relish 2½m+*

Bouvreuil (Fr)   h133 c142+

5 b.g. Saddler Maker (Ire) – Madame Lys (Fr) (Sheyrann)
2015/16 h16.4d c15.5d⁵ c19.2s* c16.4g⁵ c20.4g² c19.9d⁴ Apr 7

The respective racing colours of owner Chris Giles and Jared Sullivan (Potensis Bloodstock Ltd) both feature the colour pink, so it's rather fitting that they should share a horse whose name comes from the French for bullfinch, a smallish bird with a pinkish breast. Potensis Bloodstock Ltd sold a number of its horses at Goffs in August as part of its scaling back of its jumps racing commitments but not Bouvreuil, who showed very useful form as a novice chaser last term, including when a close second at the Cheltenham Festival for the second year running, and looks the type to land a big handicap chase this season.

The ex-French Bouvreuil produced a string of creditable efforts in his opening campaign in Britain in 2014/15, including a third to subsequent Kingwell Hurdle winner Rayvin Black on his debut for Paul Nicholls and a second in the Fred Winter at the Festival. Bouvreuil returned to action last season with a low-key effort in the Greatwood Hurdle but was quickly switched to fences, given a considerate ride on his chasing debut in the Grade 2 Henry VIII Novices' at Sandown and then winning a five-runner novice at Doncaster in January. Bouvreuil flopped on his next start returned to Grade 2 company at the same track, but the form of his victory had been franked by runner-up Vyta du Roc by the time he made his handicap debut off a mark of 139 in the Close Brothers Novices' Handicap Chase at Cheltenham. Bouvreuil produced a career best as he went down only to another improver in Ballyalton. Bouvreuil was below form in the Manifesto at Aintree on his final start—which does raise a bit of a question about his consistency—but we do feel the small field worked against him there. It's clear Bouvreuil is well-suited by the demands of big fields, and the BetVictor Gold Cup over his optimum trip of two and a half miles could be a good fit for him in the early part of the season; his trainer won it in 2012 and 2014. ***Paul Nicholls***

Conclusion: *Showed very useful form as a novice chaser at up to 2½m last term and can land a big handicap this season, possibly the BetVictor Gold Cup; goes well in big fields and has finished runner-up at the last two Cheltenham Festivals*

Phil Turner, Jumps Handicapper (Bouvreuil): *"In many ways Bouvreuil has been a frustrating customer so far, with an awkward head carriage hinting at the odd temperament quirk, whilst a record of just one win from ten starts on British soil is a paltry return for one of his ability. However, he very much looks the part for chasing and, having had another summer on his back, I'm hoping he'll prove a significant force in valuable handicap company this autumn and winter."*

Briery Belle   h134

7 b.m. King's Theatre (Ire) – Briery Ann (Anshan)
2015/16 h16.4d h20.3s³ h20.7v* h24.4s² h20.3g* Apr 14

Some horses take little or no time to realise their potential, whereas others take longer for things to click into place. It's been a case of the latter with Briery Belle. She finished only mid-field on her two starts in bumpers and then took seven goes before getting off the mark over hurdles in a mares' maiden at Huntingdon in January. Briery Belle clearly appreciated the strong test (heavy ground) over the twenty-one furlong trip that day and her stepping up to three miles in a listed mares' novice at Doncaster on her next outing had been long overdue. Briery Belle duly took another step forward, a big one in form terms in fact, and was rather unfortunate to bump into The Organist who was on a steep upward curve herself. Rather surprisingly given the way she'd been staying on in her races, Briery Belle was switched back to hold-up tactics that day and it proved counterproductive, for all she might have struggled to have beaten the winner ridden differently. Given what we've said about her being a stayer, it perhaps seems contradictory that Briery Belle was able to produce another career-best performance back over two and a half miles and away from the mud (good ground) when winning a listed mares' handicap at Cheltenham in April by three lengths from Debdebdeb, but that just highlights that she's a mare who has well and truly found her feet, and we expect to see even better from her in the new season, when she can win a mares' Grade 3 hurdle at the very least. **Henry Daly**

Conclusion: *Ended 2015/16 with a flourish, winning a listed mares' handicap hurdle at Cheltenham; that was over 2½m but she already stays 3m and will probably get further, while she's effective on ground ranging from good to heavy*

Brio Conti (Fr)   b97+

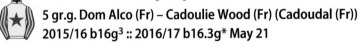

5 gr.g. Dom Alco (Fr) – Cadoulie Wood (Fr) (Cadoudal (Fr))
2015/16 b16g³ :: 2016/17 b16.3g* May 21

Silviniaco Conti has more or less put a copyright symbol on the 'Conti' moniker over the past half a dozen years, but his younger stablemate Brio Conti can still make a name for himself in the new season, when he should develop into a useful novice hurdler at the least.

A very slow pace meant the eleven runners for the bumper on the card at Warwick on April 21st only started to thin out in the home straight, but Brio Conti still managed to pull clear with two others (Clondaw Cracker and Asum) in the final two furlongs and ultimately shaped with plenty of promise. Brio Conti went two places better in a similar race at Stratford four weeks later, doing so only by a nose from Whats Not To Like but he'd probably have been an unfortunate loser as he looked by the far the best horse in the race for most of the way, leading on the bridle before the straight and quickening clear two furlongs out only to run green late on. Brio Conti found extra when asked for it by Sam Twiston-Davies and almost certainly won with something up his sleeve. Brio Conti's form is largely untested at the time of writing, but there's no reason to think it isn't solid and he looks a good prospect for his top yard, one that has had plenty of success with the progeny of Dom Alco—he's the sire of the aforementioned Silviniaco Conti, as well as Neptune Collonges, Al Ferof and Unioniste. Brio Conti is out of the French hurdles winner Cadoulie Wood, which makes him a half-brother to the French hurdler/chaser Coco Wood, and he should make a good impression on the two-mile novice hurdling scene in the coming months. **Paul Nicholls**

Conclusion: *Showed plenty of ability in two bumper starts and should make a name for himself as a novice hurdler; appears to have enough pace for 2m though may well stay further*

 ## Captain Chaos (Ire) h134

5 ch.g. Golan (Ire) – Times Have Changed (Ire) (Safety Catch (USA))
2015/16 h15.8v* h19.8v^2 h20.3v h18.5v* h18.9v^2 Mar 30

Captain Chaos was the alter-ego of the mild-mannered mechanic Victor Prinzim in the *Cannonball Run* movie series and his arrival in times of need was signalled by the now famous musical accompaniment: "*Dun dun dunn!*" Whether such a gesture will ever be adopted to celebrate the presence of the equine Captain Chaos on a racecourse is questionable, but the five-year-old certainly has plenty of natural ability himself, and he should be able to build on his very encouraging first season over hurdles in the new campaign.

A wide-margin winner of a Newcastle bumper for Tim Fitzgerald in January 2015, Captain Chaos had joined Dan Skelton by the time he made his hurdling debut at Uttoxeter last November. Captain Chaos made hard work of justifying odds of 2/1-on that day, but he still gave the impression he would come on for the experience and he duly improved when runner-up to Label des Obeaux in the following month's Grade 2 Winter Novices' Hurdle at Sandown. Captain Chaos shaped as if something was amiss when down the field at Cheltenham on New Year's Day, but he quickly bounced back to regain the winning thread in a novice at Exeter, admittedly not needing to produce his best to again land the odds. He then ran creditably when signing off over at Enghien in France in March, finishing second in a valuable minor event won by his main market rival Ozamo.

Captain Chaos will be suited by the return to two and a half miles (and further) and looks one of the most interesting prospects for good-quality handicap hurdles in

2016/17. The lengthy, raw-boned Captain Chaos looks the type who'll take to chasing too, though it's probably worth pointing out he's still only five so far from guaranteed to be sent over fences this season. *Dan Skelton*

Conclusion: *Won twice as a novice last term (also runner-up in Grade 2) and should make an even bigger name for himself this season, be it over hurdles (BHA mark of 139) or fences; should prove suited by a return to 2½m+*

Clan des Obeaux (Fr) ★   h143p

4 b.g. Kapgarde (Fr) – Nausicaa des Obeaux (Fr) (April Night (Fr))
2015/16 h16.3v* h16.8v^2 h16.8g^6 Mar 18

The aforementioned Bouvreuil and the year-younger Clan des Obeaux probably know each other well, as they both began their careers with French trainer Nicolas Devilder before joining Paul Nicholls. One difference between them is that while Bouvreuil took nine starts to get off the mark (including two runs on the Flat), Clan des Obeaux scored at the first time of asking in a bumper at La Roche-Sur-Yon (no? it has a chocolate museum if you fancy it) in April 2015. Subsequently purchased by Paul Barber and Potensis Bloodstock Ltd and transferred to Nicholls, Clan des Obeaux made a most taking hurdling debut after eight months off in a juvenile at Newbury just before Christmas, drawing twenty-one lengths clear of the now 130-rated Jaleo. After that performance, Nicholls said: "He's a very, very smart horse," before adding "I'm going to have to be very persuasive [with his owners] to run him in the Triumph." Clan des Obeaux had his Festival prep race in the Grade 2 Finesse Novices' at Cheltenham in late-January and, while he was turned over at 11/8f, he was a big eye-catcher as he almost certainly pressed on too soon (went 1.06 in-running on Betfair) and there was no disgrace in losing to Protek des Flos (also owned by Potentis, incidentally) anyway. Nicholls got his wish and Clan des Obeaux lined up as a 12/1-shot for the Triumph Hurdle, but he wasn't seen to best effect on the fastest ground he'd encountered over timber (both previous efforts on heavy) and ran just respectably as he finished sixth of fifteen to Ivanovich Gorbatov.

Though many say beauty is in the eye of the beholder, Clan des Obeaux is clearly like the equine equivalent of David Gandy—our own reporters say he's a 'well-made gelding who looks the part', while his trainer describes him as "a gorgeous looking horse who will make an awesome chaser". Given Clan des Obeaux's scope for physical improvement over the summer, a hurdles mark of 139 looks 'workable' (as all trainers say about a horse they know is well handicapped), though it will be no surprise to see him sent over the larger obstacles sooner rather than later. *Paul Nicholls*

Conclusion: *Showed form bordering on smart in light novice hurdle campaign in 2015/16 and can climb even higher this term, whether he's kept over hurdles or switched to chasing (even as a four-year-old); best form so far on heavy ground*

Cloudy Dream (Ire) h141p

6 gr.g. Cloudings (Ire) – Run Away Dream (Ire) (Acceglio)
2015/16 b17.1m* h16.2s³ h19.5g* h18.6s* h16d² Apr 16

Have you ever wondered where the inspiration for a good portion of the cloud-based collection of racehorse names comes from? The answer is the French sire Cloudings. Cloudings was trained by Andre Fabre to win the Group 1 Prix Lupin over the extended ten furlongs at Longchamp, but since going to stud in 1999 he's become much better known for his jumpers than his Flat performers. The pick of Cloudings' National Hunt progeny are Many Clouds, whose wins include the Hennessy and Grand National, Cloudy Lane, who won the Peter Marsh and Aintree Fox Hunters', and Cloudy Too, who also won the Peter Marsh. After going very close to winning the Scottish Champion Hurdle as a novice last term, it's anticipated that Cloudy Dream can win a big race of his own this season.

Cloudy Dream won two of his three starts in bumpers, including on his return last October, and he also won two of his first three outings over hurdles, namely a novice at Doncaster in November and an open handicap at Market Rasen four months later. Cloudy Dream then produced a very eye-catching second to Ch'tibello in the Scottish Champion Hurdle at Ayr, the victim of a rare lapse in judgement by his rider Noel Fehily who lost his position on the gelding and left him with plenty to do approaching the final flight. That form worked out well over the summer too, with the third Clondaw Warrior winning the Galway Hurdle and the fifth Ivan Grozny winning the Grimes Hurdle. A 4 lb rise (to 137) looks very fair for Cloudy Dream and he should have a good handicap in him if kept over hurdles in the new season, though given he's owned by Trevor Hemmings it would be no surprise to see him transferred to chasing. We feel he should excel in that sphere too, as he's a good-topped gelding out of a half-sister to the high-class two-mile chaser Get Real. Cloudy Dream's trainer Malcom Jefferson has also done well over fences with another son of Cloudings in Sun Cloud, who has won four times over the larger obstacles and finished sixth in the 2016 Scottish Grand National at 40/1. *Malcolm Jefferson*

Conclusion: *Impressed in first campaign over hurdles last term, winning an open handicap and finishing an eye-catching second in strong Scottish Champion Hurdle; has a big handicap hurdle in him, though appeals as very much the sort to make a chaser too; effective from 2m to 2½m*

Coeur Blimey (Ire)   b115

5 b.g. Winged Love (Ire) – Eastender (Opening Verse (USA))
2015/16 b15.7d* b16.4g :: 2016/17 b16d Apr 27

When Coeur Blimey won the listed bumper at Ascot's Long Walk Hurdle meeting last December he achieved a feat the likes of King's Palace (runner-up in 2012), Yanworth and Thistlecrack (second and fifth in 2014) had all failed to accomplish. What's more, he pulled clear with one other horse—the subsequent Champion Bumper winner Ballyandy.

Granted, Coeur Blimey was receiving 4 lb from Ballyandy that day, and he failed to match the form in either the Champion Bumper at Cheltenham (eleventh) or Punchestown (eighth to Blow By Blow), but that Ascot performance (smart on the Timeform scale) cannot be taken away from him. One big attraction to Coeur Blimey is his stable which, while capable, will almost certainly mean he starts at a bigger price for some novice hurdles than he should do, certainly based on his bumper form. Coeur Blimey has the pedigree to take to jumping too, as he's by the sire of Hunt Ball, Josses Hill and Bless The Wings out of a half-sister to the very smart hurdler and fairly useful chaser Westender. He's also a full brother to the fairly useful hurdler Just Get Cracking. Just Get Cracking stays twenty-one furlongs, while Westender stayed three miles, and Coeur Blimey will likely stay beyond two miles himself this season, when he has the potential to take quite high rank in the novice hurdle division for his small but able yard. ***Susan Gardner***

Conclusion: *Beat subsequent Cheltenham Champion Bumper winner Ballyandy in December and, while well held in Grade 1s thereafter, looks a top prospect for novice hurdles*

Drumcliff (Ire)   b101 h113p

5 b.g. Presenting – Dusty Too (Terimon)
2015/16 b16.5s* b16g³ h16s Mar 28

Including a horse that finished last of eight on its only previous start over jumps in this list is obviously risky, but there are a number of factors that suggest Drumcliff will prove much better than he showed that day, not least his very eye-catching pedigree. Drumcliff is a half-brother to none other than the high-class hurdler/top-class chaser Simonsig, and the fact his aforementioned hurdling debut came in the Grade 2 Rathbarry & Glenview Studs Novices' at Fairyhouse's Irish Grand National meeting in late-March highlights the regard in which he must be held by his trainer Harry Fry and owner J. P. McManus.

Drumcliff was left behind from three out in that race won by Sutton Place, but he was not given at all a hard time by his rider Mark Walsh once his winning chance had gone and he should have learnt plenty from the experience. What's more, Drumcliff had previously looked a good prospect in bumpers. He was strong in the betting (7/4) ahead of his debut in a newcomers bumper at Taunton last December and created a fine impression as he won by five lengths and more from three next-time-out winners, among them the runner-up Capitaine who won a similar race at Wincanton when next seen four months later by thirteen lengths and is now rated 114. Drumcliff was beaten into third behind Bolving and Templeross carrying a penalty in a similar event at Kempton eleven weeks later, but he was patently still green, and he still looked a horse who would be worth following in 2016/17.

Drumcliff understandably wasn't cheap, costing €60,000 as a three-year-old, but that could still prove money well spent given his potential. He's raced at two miles so far, but it would be no surprise if he stayed further in time given his pedigree (by the same sire as Gold Cup winners Denman and War of Attrition out a mare who won at up to twenty-one furlongs over hurdles). **Harry Fry**

Conclusion: *Last of eight on his hurdling debut but that came in an Irish Grade 2 and he'd previously looked a good prospect in bumpers; half-brother to Simonsig and should improve plenty over timber this season*

Emerging Force (Ire)   h144p

6 b.g. Milan – Danette (Ger) (Exit To Nowhere (USA))
2015/16 h19.1s* h18.8v³ h24.4d* h22.8gᵘʳ :: 2016/17 h24dᵖᵘ Apr 27

'Harry Whittington is a name you should make yourselves very familiar with' read a line in the Future Stars chapter of *Horses to Follow 2013/14* and, though our prediction was perhaps a shade premature given Whittington saddled just two winners that season, we now feel vindicated after the trainer won twenty-one races last term. Whittington gained his big breakthrough with Grade 1-winning novice chaser Arzal in 2015/16 and, while that horse sadly had to be put down in April, the same connections do have another promising young horse on their hands in the aptly-named Emerging Force.

Emerging Force ended last season on something of a low note after unseating in a handicap at Haydock and pulled up in a Grade 1 at Punchestown, but he was around three lengths up when unshipping Nico de Boinville at the final flight in the former race and was consequently sent off at only 6/1 for the latter. Emerging Force had made a winning debut in a Fontwell maiden hurdle (from subsequent dual winner Hit The Highway) in November and, after losing out in a battle for the lead on heavy ground at Newbury next time, he got back to winning ways in an open handicap at Doncaster in February. Emerging Force won by just a nose (from Whataknight) on Town Moor but he did beat eighteen rivals, finding plenty to do so upped to three miles, and it was no surprise to see him to produce an even better performance (or at least he would have done had he completed) at Haydock. Emerging Force remains on a fair BHA mark of 146 (6 lb higher than Haydock) and will head into 2016/17 with plenty of potential still intact. **Harry Whittington**

Conclusion: *Made great strides last season and was set to win the Stayers Hurdle Series Final at Haydock prior to unseating at the last; forgiven pulled-up effort in Punchestown Grade 1 on final start and interesting for handicaps over 2¾m+*

Flying Angel (Ire) h143

5 gr.g. Arcadio (Ger) – Gypsy Kelly (Ire) (Roselier (Fr))
2015/16 h20g* h20s² h17v³ h21d⁵ h16.3v³ h16s* h20.3g² h20s³ :: 2016/17 c20s* Sep 22

Wrapping in cotton wool isn't something associated with Nigel Twiston-Davies' approach to training, and there could be no better example during last season than Flying Angel, who first reached the racecourse in October and made his final appearance almost six months—and seven outings—later in April. But as with many that have gone

Flying Angel wins the Imperial Cup at Sandown

before, the trainer's proactive approach reaped rich dividends, as Flying Angel thrived on racing, supplementing his debut win (at Worcester) with success in the Imperial Cup in March, just a month after a fine third in the Betfair Hurdle at Newbury and less than a week before another sterling handicap performance in the Martin Pipe at the Cheltenham Festival, when finding only Ibis du Rheu too good in a twenty-four strong field. Flying Angel's third to Yorkhill in the Grade 1 Mersey Novices' Hurdle at Aintree on his final outing wasn't too shabby, either.

Flying Angel did more in half a year than the majority of racehorses manage in their whole careers, and his reputation is set to be bolstered still further in 2016/17 judging by his successful chasing debut at Perth last month, where he travelled strongly before cruising clear. An enthusiastic, good-topped gelding out of a Roselier mare, Flying Angel will be well worth his place in stronger company. **Nigel Twiston-Davies**

Conclusion: *Made giant strides in his first season, winning the Imperial Cup in between placed efforts in two other famous handicaps, and also finishing third to Yorkhill in Aintree Grade 1; built for fences and has the scope to improve on his hurdling exploits*

 ## Go Long (Ire)   h135p

6 b.g. Hurricane Run (Ire) – Monumental Gesture (Head For Heights)
2015/16 h16.6g* h19.5d² Dec 29

It's still early for Hurricane Run to be classified as a failure at stud, his oldest progeny still only eight after all, but it's fair to say that his early crops have been a bit short on high-quality performers, with the 2014 Prix Niel winner Ectot being his best Flat runner on Timeform ratings. He's certainly yet to sire a jumper that's really made the grade, but maybe Go Long will be the one to put that right, already the best of them after just two outings over hurdles.

As a good-looking half-brother to the top-class hurdler Rhinestone Cowboy and smart hurdler/chaser Wichita Lineman it was always on the cards that Go Long would fetch plenty at the sales, and he was knocked down to The Ruckers for a cool £150,000 after finishing second of three finishers in an Irish maiden point on his debut as a five-year-old. Go Long has obviously got a long way to go before he even starts to justify that sort of outlay, but he's been campaigned so far as though connections believe he's got plenty of long-term potential, considerably handled in a bumper before accounting for the smart Charbel in a novice over the extended two miles at Doncaster on his hurdling debut. On the face of it, it was maybe a bit disappointing that Go Long failed to improve when favourite under a penalty for a similar race over three furlongs further there a month later, but he again shaped encouragingly and the fact he wasn't seen out again is probably indicative of connections taking a long-term view with him.

In time, there seems little doubt that fences should bring out the best in Go Long, but an opening BHA mark of 134 over hurdles means he'll surely be interesting in the short term, too, remaining with a fair amount of room for improvement after just four outings in all spheres so far. **Evan Williams**

Conclusion: *Half-brother to the top-class hurdler Rhinestone Cowboy and smart hurdler/chaser Wichita Lineman who can repay his connections for their patience this season; on an attractive mark of 134 over hurdles, while he'll make a chaser further down the line*

Gully's Edge   h132p

6 b.g. Kayf Tara – Shuildante (Ire) (Phardante (Fr))
2015/16 b16.5d² b17.1g³ h25.3v² h23.3s* h24.3s* Apr 15

Gully's Edge, unlike England's slip cordon in the recent Test series against Pakistan, didn't need much practice last season, breaking his duck on just his second start over hurdles in a novice at Hexham in late-March. Gully's Edge's full brother Lord Larsson, a fairly useful hurdler/chaser who was also trained by Malcolm Jefferson, won wearing a tongue tie and Gully's Edge sported the same equipment for his first three starts in bumpers (placed on each occasion) and also on his final outing last season, when he followed up his Hexham win in a novice handicap at Ayr. After breaks of six months, three months and two and a half months prior to each of his three previous runs, it was encouraging to see Gully's Edge prove he doesn't need long spells between his races when winning at Ayr, which came following just seventeen days off. Gully's Edge showed useful form when making a winning handicap debut at Ayr, coming five lengths clear of his nearest pursuer Caledonia under 5-lb claimer Jamie Hamilton, and with further improvement to come, he can win again off his new mark of 135 (up 9lb). That said, he's a big, strapping individual who we see very much as a staying novice chaser this term, and provided he takes to the new discipline, he has the potential to clean up in such races over three miles and beyond in the North this winter. Gully's Edge clearly goes well on soft going, both his wins having come on such a surface, though his trainer still believes he "will be better suited by genuine good ground." **Malcolm Jefferson**

Conclusion: *Proved he doesn't need a long break between races with final win last season and could mop up in novice chases in the North; will stay further than 3m*

Hell's Kitchen ★ h132

5 b.g. Robin des Champs (Fr) – Mille Et Une (Fr) (Trempolino (USA))
2015/16 h16s³ h20.5v* h20.5d² Apr 1

The irony of a horse called Hell's Kitchen being trained by a man named Fry. Hell's Kitchen showed useful form in just three starts over hurdles last season and would win more races if kept over timber, but he's set to switch to chasing this term and appeals as the sort to do very well in that discipline given he's a big, well-made gelding by the same sire as Vautour and Sir des Champs out of a sister to the useful chaser Madox.

Hell's Kitchen was beaten over twenty lengths when third of ten on his debut in a novice hurdle on soft ground at Kempton in January, but that form would prove strong (beaten by Wait For Me and Querry Horse) and he readily went two places better in a similar race on heavy going at Newbury five weeks later, doing so by two lengths from Walking In The Air. Hell's Kitchen jumped and travelled well before taking things up before the final hurdle and going on to win readily. Hell's Kitchen's profile was dented slightly when he was turned over at 3/1-on in another novice at Newbury a month later, beaten nine lengths into second of six behind Bigbadjohn, but on good to soft ground and with the winner making all, he was unsuited by the relative speed test at the trip and is definitely worth another chance. We suspect Hell's Kitchen's career has merely been bubbling under so far and he's taken to win a good race or two over fences in the coming months; he's certainly in very good hands to fulfil his potential. *Harry Fry*

Conclusion: *Showed useful form in a light campaign over hurdles in 2015/16 and should prove at least as effective as a novice chaser this term; stays a testing 2½m*

Herons Heir (Ire) h111 c123p

8 b.g. Heron Island (Ire) – Kyle Lamp (Ire) (Miner's Lamp)
2015/16 h15.6s⁵ h16.7v³ h16.7v* h17.7s h15.8d² h16.8s² :: 2016/17 c16g*
c16.3gᶠ c15.8d⁵ Jun 10

The Highclere Thoroughbred Racing website emphatically states: 'Each shareowner acknowledges that participation in the syndicates is for the purpose of sharing in the enjoyment of the horses and NOT FOR INVESTMENT.' Those fortunate enough to be involved in the ownership of eight-year-old Herons Heir might not have made a financial profit from his two wins and three placed efforts over jumps since being brought from his previous connections (for whom he won a Wexford bumper) for £90,000, but they will have enjoyed themselves nonetheless, especially when the gelding ran out a four-and-a-half-length winner of a novices' handicap on his chasing debut at Warwick in May.

Prior to that, Herons Heir had left his previous hurdling efforts behind to open his account on his handicap debut at Market Rasen in January, wearing a first-time tongue tie and settling better than had often been the case. Herons Heir finished second in two more handicap hurdles in April before switching to fences, following in the footsteps of his half-brother Got The Urge who was a long-standing maiden over hurdles but won twice over the larger obstacles. Herons Heir blotted his copybook with a heavy fall five out at Fakenham twenty days later in May, and his jumping again deserted him when it mattered when fifth of eight in an open handicap at Aintree in June. However, it had looked an asset at Warwick and it's hoped that some intensive schooling over the summer will help him get back on track. Herons Heir certainly remains a well-handicapped chaser on a mark of 123 given the runner-up at Warwick won next time. **Dan Skelton**

Conclusion: *Jumping fell apart on final two starts last season but it had looked an asset when he made a winning chasing debut; in good hands to get back on track and can land a valuable 2m handicap chase*

 ## Imperial Prince (Ire)   h119p

7 b.g. Subtle Power (Ire) – Satco Rose (Ire) (Satco (Fr))
2015/16 h16d h16.4s h19.4s³ h20.6v* h22.7d* Apr 11

Given he's bred for stamina—by the sire of Haydock Grand National Trial winner Lie Forrit out of a full sister to useful three-mile hurdler/chaser Satco Express—it was predictable that Imperial Prince would thrive for the step up to two and a half miles and further earlier this year, and another increased stamina test is bound to bring about more improvement this season.

Imperial Prince raced in bumpers for Michael Smith before joining Sandy Thomson, for whom he won open handicap hurdles at Newcastle and Kelso this spring, again travelling well but still appreciating the step up to two and three-quarters miles when beating next-time-out winner Maggie Blue in the latter race. Imperial Prince defied an 11 lb rise in the weights that day, and we feel he'll have no trouble overcoming another 8 lb hike (to 120) this campaign, though any success won't be for Thomson as the gelding was bought by trainer Charlie Longsdon at the recent Horses In Training Sale at Goffs UK (Doncaster). Longsdon has clearly bought a horse with potential still untapped, and we're sure he'll get plenty more out of him in the coming months, with the step up to three miles likely to come sooner rather than later. **Charlie Longsdon**

Conclusion: *Form took off once stepped up to 2½m and switched to handicaps last term and should win more handicap hurdles for new stable this time around; will stay 3m and acts on heavy going*

It'safreebee (Ire) h146

6 b.g. Danroad (AUS) – Aphra Benn (Ire) (In The Wings)
2015/16 b18v⁴ b17g³ b17.2s* b16s² h16.7v* h18.9v* h15.7v* h21.1g³ Mar 16

From a numerical point of view, Dan Skelton will have seen last season as a great triumph as he broke the hundred-winner mark in Britain for the first time since getting his first full licence in 2013. But it wasn't just a numbers game for the trainer, as his haul featured plenty of quality too, with Ch'tibello landing the Scottish Champion Hurdle and Superb Story providing Skelton with his first Cheltenham Festival winner in the County Hurdle. What the 'hundred winners' or 'first Festival winner' headlines don't highlight, however, is just how well Skelton's other runners at the 2016 Cheltenham Festival fared. Quite frankly, as a collective they ran out of their skins, with six of the fifteen—predictably including Superb Story—producing career-best performances on Timeform ratings.

Another of the sextet was Its'afreebee who belied odds of 33/1 to finish third in the Neptune Novices' Hurdle behind market principals Yorkhill and Yanworth. That was another improved effort from Its'afreebee who had made a winning hurdling debut at Bangor in November for Irish trainer Mark Fahey (who'd also saddled him to finish in the first four on each of his four bumper outings, including a win). Its'afreebee had then made a successful first start for Skelton with a twenty-four length stroll over nineteen furlongs at Haydock just after Christmas, before completing his hat-trick in the Grade 2 Rossington Main Novices' Hurdle dropped back to two miles there almost a month later. Its'afreebee showed a really likeable attitude when seeing off Le Prezien (won a similar race next time) by three-quarters of a length for his final success, and that's sure to stand him in good stead in the future. Its'afreebee also has the physique of one who will do well over fences this season, when he will hopefully develop into a very smart sort at up to two and a half miles. All three of Its'afreebee's hurdles win were achieved on heavy ground, but he proved at the Festival that he doesn't need the mud. *Dan Skelton*

Conclusion: *Likeable front runner who built on Grade 2 novice hurdle win when third behind Yorkhill and Yanworth in the Neptune at Cheltenham; looks a chaser (ran twice in points) and should prove one to follow if switched to fences this term*

Jenkins (Ire) ★ b116+

4 b.g. Azamour (Ire) – Aladiyna (Ire) (Indian Danehill (Ire))
2015/16 b16.3g* :: 2016/17 b16d² Apr 26

Ballyandy and Blow By Blow, the respective winners of the Champion Bumpers at Cheltenham and Punchestown, shared the accolade of being Timeform's highest-rated performers in the division last season, closely followed by Aintree's Champion Bumper winner Bacardys. However, those horses ran to their peak ratings after having had at least two prior starts, and none of their debut efforts were rated as highly as the performance produced by Jenkins when he destroyed a big field in a Newbury bumper in April on his first start. Jenkins' nine-length win over Cash Again—himself a good prospect for Paul Nicholls and J. P. McManus this season (had won his only previous start in France for Guy Cherel)—led to him being sent off at 11/8-on for the valuable Goffs Land Rover Bumper at the Punchestown Festival. Though Jenkins couldn't reproduce his debut form and was beaten half a length by Coeur de Lion, he did go like the best horse at the weights (touched 1.03 in-running on Betfair) until being collared well inside the final furlong. The pair pulled seven lengths clear of the third and it looks strong form.

While Jenkins was bred primarily for the Flat—his half-brother O'kelly Hammer won between six furlongs and a mile and a quarter in France—his sire Azamour has enjoyed National Hunt success with the likes of Zarkandar and Third Intention, while his dam Aladiyna is a half-sister to the smart two-mile hurdler Alaivan. Jenkins doesn't lack physical scope either, so there's no obvious reason why he shouldn't take well to hurdling and we see him as the type to win graded novices at two miles this season. **Nicky Henderson**

Conclusion: *Produced the best performance by a debutant in a bumper all last season when winning by nine lengths at Newbury in April; turned over in Ireland next time but went like the best horse for a long way and is very much one to look out for in 2m novice hurdles this term*

 Kayf Grace b115

6 b.m. Kayf Tara – Potter's Gale (Ire) (Strong Gale)
2015/16 b16.6g² b16v* b17s* Apr 7

Beating another animal who ranks highly in the minds of the Timeform Editorial department isn't a rite of passage into the *Fifty*, but it doesn't half help.

Augusta Kate has been well regarded by the Editorial collective ever since her debut rout at Listowel last September, and she set the form standard down in grade when she lined up for Aintree's Grade 2 mares' bumper in April. It says plenty for the strides Kayf Grace was making last spring, therefore, that she got the better of the Willie Mullins-trained favourite that day, with the pair dominating the latter stages and pulling clear of a whole host of useful previous winners. Kayf Grace showed a fantastic attitude under pressure to prevail by half a length and also maintained her run-to-run progress.

Kayf Grace gets the better of Augusta Kate at Aintree

Despite her 14/1 starting price, there was no fluke about Kayf Grace's success, and this extremely well-bred mare—she's from one of the best jumps families in the book as she's out of the useful hurdler/winning chaser Potter's Gale, who is a half-sister to Denman—promises to make hay in novice hurdles this season, especially against her own sex. Kayf Grace will definitely stay further than two miles, though her Aintree performance—not to mention her fifty-length win at Fakenham the time before—underlined she's by no means short of speed. **Nicky Henderson**

Conclusion: *Developed into a smart bumper performer last term and should make similar strides over hurdles; will stay further than 2m but clearly isn't short of speed*

Keep Up Keira (Ire) h83p

5 b.m. Scorpion (Ire) – Perspex Queen (Ire) (Presenting)
2015/16 b16g⁵ b15.8s⁴ h15.3v⁶ h21.2g :: 2016/17 h16m⁵ May 16

It's unusual for a horse to make the jumps version of *Horses to Follow* with a lower Timeform Rating than most of those included in the same year's Flat book, but despite her lowly figure, Keep Up Keira has shown enough to suggest she could be worth following this season.

Bred for stamina—her dam was a winning pointer, out of a half-sister to the dam of high-class three-mile chaser Strong Flow—it's not too much of a surprise that Keep Up Keira has looked in need of a stiffer test in her five starts to date at up to twenty-one furlongs (bumpers and hurdles). Keep Up Keira also looks to have been brought along with handicaps firmly in mind, again catching the eye when a staying-on (albeit well-held) fifth of twelve to Master of Speed on her qualifying run at Kempton last time. Keep Up Keira's opening mark of 96 is stiff enough on the bare form of what she's achieved to date, but she's expected to improve plenty when switched to more suitable races by her shrewd trainer Neil Mulholland. It may even be that she's capable of racking up a sequence. **Neil Mulholland**

Conclusion: *Not shown much in form terms but has caught the eye with a view to switching to handicaps and stepping up beyond 21f*

Knockgraffon (Ire) h129

6 b.g. Flemensfirth (USA) – Gleaming Spire (Overbury (Ire))
2015/16 h20g² h20.5d* h20.5v² h16s h18.5s* Mar 26

Three Musketeers provided Dan Skelton with the biggest win of his career—from a race status point of view—up until that point when winning the Grade 2 Leamington Novices' Hurdle at Warwick in January 2015. The gelding is another good advert for Flemensfirth, a sire Skelton has enjoyed particular success with since taking out his training licence in 2013 (we've already included a Skelton-trained son of Flemensfirth in this list in Bekkensfirth). The Barbara Hester-owned pair of Walking In The Air and Knockgraffon are two more promising horses by Flemensfirth currently under Skelton's care, and the latter in particular is expected to make his presence felt in some good-quality handicap hurdles at around two and a half miles this season.

Knockgraffon was placed in two bumpers—including for Irish trainer Timmy Hyde—before being sent over hurdles at Aintree last October, when he finished two and three-quarter lengths second to Perform (and a place in front of next-time-out winner American). Knockgraffon opened his account in a novice at Leicester the following month and then finished a good second to Hit The Highway there in January.

Knockgraffon finished only mid-field in a typically competitive renewal of the Imperial Cup at Sandown in March, but the drop back to two miles might have been against him, and he got straight back on the up when recording a wide-margin success back in novice company at Market Rasen. The useful-looking Knockgraffon is ultimately a chaser—and would clearly warrant significant interest if going down that route this term—but he also remains with potential as a hurdler and could yet prove himself favourably treated off a mark of 132. **Dan Skelton**

Conclusion: *Future chaser, but can land a good-quality hurdle at around 2½m this term*

Minella Rocco (Ire) ★   c153p

6 b.g. Shirocco (Ger) – Petralona (USA) (Alleged (USA))
2015/16 c21.6v³ c25.3sᵖᵘ c20.8v⁶ c23.8s² c31.8g* Mar 15

Early on in the National Hunt Chase Challenge Cup at the latest Cheltenham Festival, top Irish amateur Derek O'Connor might have been thinking he had made a mistake in passing up the ride on Colin Tizzard's Native River. He'd instead opted for the Jonjo

Minella Rocco heads the eventual third Measureofmydeams in the four-miler

O'Neill-trained and J.P. McManus-owned Minella Rocco, and the big gelding had put in a couple of sticky jumps and was trailing the field for most of the first circuit. However, Minella Rocco warmed to the task as the race wore on and O'Connor, who'd ridden a double at the Festival in 2011 and who has well over one thousand point-to-point winners to his name in Ireland, produced his mount into contention steadily as Minella Rocco's stamina came into play late on and they went on to score by one and a quarter lengths from the aforementioned Native River. The victory was a sixth in the race for O'Neill and a fifth for McManus, with the pair also combining successfully in 2002 with Rith Dubh, whose rider J. T. McNamara sadly passed away this July aged forty-one.

Minella Rocco had failed to win in his first four starts over fences and there's a feeling that there's room for improvement in the jumping department, but he's still a raw recruit to some degree and could yet make an even bigger impact, with long-distance handicaps the obvious route with him—indeed, he looks a prime candidate for the Grand Nationals at Fairyhouse and Aintree. *Jonjo O'Neill*

Conclusion: *Winner of the 4m National Hunt Chase at Cheltenham in his first season over fences and looks set to play a big part in the top-staying chase handicaps this time around; looks worth a long-range bet at 33/1 for the Grand National*

 ### Moon Racer (Ire)   b122+ h125P
7 b.g. Saffron Walden (Fr) – Angel's Folly (Wesaam (USA))
2015/16 NR :: 2016/17 b16d² h16s* Sep 22

Although there have clearly been problems along the way—which prevented him playing an active part among our *Fifty* for 2015/16, with his sole run coming in Ireland after the British season had officially ended—David Pipe's Moon Racer still looks one of the most exciting hurdling recruits around. Purchased by his current connections for £225,000 after landing a Fairyhouse bumper, Moon Racer won his next two starts at Cheltenham, latterly justifying favouritism in the Champion Bumper at the Festival.

Moon Racer was favourite for the Supreme Novices' Hurdle at the latest Cheltenham Festival when injury ruled him out in November, but he returned in the Punchestown Champion Bumper in April and looked at least as good as ever in going down by three-quarters of a length to Blow By Blow. Moon Racer looked the likely winner for much of the straight, too, only for Blow By Blow to pull out more.

Moon Racer finally made his long-awaited hurdling bow in a virtual match against last season's Champion Bumper winner Ballyandy at Perth last month. Moon Racer was keen early on and novicey at times, but Pipe will have been delighted with the end result: a battling three-quarters of a length victory over his main rival. The Supreme Novices' (for which he's generally a 12/1 second favourite behind an unknown quantity from the Willie Mullins yard called Senewalk) is likely the main aim after what happened last season. **David Pipe**

Conclusion: *Obviously been hard to train but proved as good as ever on belated return when second to Blow By Blow in Champion Bumper at Punchestown in April; should prove a leading contender for top novice hurdle honours with a clear run, probably over 2m for all he's likely to stay further*

Mount Mews (Ire)   b113p

5 b.g. Presenting – Kneeland Lass (Ire) (Bob Back (USA))
2015/16 b16.7v* :: 2016/17 b16.2d* May 4

The fact that Mount Mews has won both his starts in bumpers by a combined total of twelve and a half lengths bodes very well for his future, as he's bred to be a staying chaser being by Presenting out of a full sister to the high-class staying chaser Burton Port. Mount Mews was relatively unfancied in the betting (10/1) for his debut in a seven-runner race at Market Rasen in April, but he stayed on well to lead entering the final furlong and pulled two and a half lengths clear of fellow newcomer Bally Gilbert. The heavy ground at Market Rasen may well have played to Mount Mews' strengths given his stamina-laden pedigree, but he proved he could handle less testing ground (good to soft) just as well when following up by a wide margin at Kelso twenty-four days later. Under a penalty, Mount Mews was conceding weight to the whole field, including the runner-up Nicholas T who won a Flat maiden on his next start before being placed in handicaps on the level off marks in the 70s. The time of the Kelso race might have been slower than the second division (won by the Nicky Henderson-trained Thomas Campbell, who should also win races over hurdles this term) as a result of a steadier pace, but the finishing sectional, taken from passing three out, was almost two seconds faster. All this means Mount Mews is an exciting prospect for novice hurdles, and he's likely to stay at least two and a half miles, so could even develop into the North's leading hope for either the Neptune or Albert Bartlett Novices' Hurdle. **Malcolm Jefferson**

Conclusion: *Bodes very well that he's won both his bumper starts in good style as he's bred to be a staying chaser (dam a full sister to Burton Port); exciting prospect for novice hurdles and likely to stay at least 2½m*

Mystifiable h111 c135p

8 gr.g. Kayf Tara – Royal Keel (Long Leave)
2015/16 h18.5g* h16.4d⁵ c20.2s* c22.4s* c25s^pu Apr 9

The Fergal O'Brien stable got back on track last season by recording thirty-three wins, with its runners earning almost as much prize money as they did during the 2013/14 season which saw Alvarado win a Grade 3 handicap chase and finish fourth in the Grand National. O'Brien will be looking to build on those totals from his newly-refurbished Upper Yard in Naunton, where he's a neighbour of his old boss Nigel Twiston-Davies.

Mystifiable was resurgent in 2015/16 himself, first of all making light of a sixteen-month absence when winning a handicap hurdle at Exeter on his return in October. Though Mystifiable had been given a chance by the handicapper prior to that success, dropped 6 lb to a mark of 107, he had little difficulty defying 112 in a handicap chase at Leicester two starts later on just his second outing over fences (and first since early-2014). Mystifiable matched his seven-length winning margin in a novice handicap at Newbury nine weeks later in March, easily overcoming another 8 lb rise in the weights from Baku Bay. Mystifiable has more stamina than his full sister Kayf Keel and half-brother Hidden Keel, both of whom found twenty-one furlongs to be their limit, but he appeared to find twenty-five furlongs on soft ground too much of a test prior to being pulled up at Aintree on his final outing. He still shaped well for a long way, though, which suggests it was indeed the trip that contributed significantly to his defeat rather than his new mark of 132. Mystifiable probably does appreciate a break between his races and he'll be one to look at on his return, though we do feel there's more mileage in him than that. *Fergal O'Brien*

Conclusion: *Won handicaps over hurdles and fences at up to 2¾m last season and can win more similar events; probably needs a fair break between his races, so first time back may be a particularly good time to back him*

Native River (Ire) c152p

6 ch.g. Indian River (Fr) – Native Mo (Ire) (Be My Native (USA))
2015/16 c19.4g³ c24.2s* c23.4s* c24d³ c24.2v³ c31.8g² c25d* Apr 8

Colin Tizzard enjoyed a remarkable 2015/16 season, with Thistlecrack dominating the staying hurdling scene by winning all his five starts, including both the World Hurdle and Liverpool Stayers' Hurdle by seven lengths. Arguably an even greater training achievement by Tizzard was his rejuvenation of Cue Card, who won the Betfair Chase, King George and Aintree Bowl after he'd ended the previous season by finishing a well-held fourth to Don Cossack in the Punchestown Gold Cup, which was actually his best performance of that campaign on Timeform ratings.

Native River and Richard Johnson make all in the Mildmay at Aintree

Tizzard's third individual Grade 1 winner last term was Native River, who won the Mildmay Novices' Chase at Aintree in April under an excellent front-running ride from Richard Johnson. Native River had looked a chaser going places when beating Un Temps Pour Tout by three and three-quarter lengths in the Grade 2 Worcester Novices' Chase at Newbury in November, and he put a couple of lazy efforts in the Kauto Star and Towton Novices' Chases behind him in first-time cheekpieces when second of twenty to Minella Rocco in the four-miler at Cheltenham in March. Native River again ran in snatches, while his jumping wasn't too great either, but he still produced a career-best effort and even better was to come. Riding the gelding for the first time, champion jockey Johnson made full use of Native River's stamina back over twenty-five furlongs in the Mildmay as the pair made all by three lengths from Henri Parry Morgan, with the recent Cheltenham Festival winners Blaklion (RSA), Un Temps Pour Tout (Ultima Handicap) and Ballyalton (Close Brothers Novices' Handicap) in third, fourth and fifth. Now connections have found the key to Native River he could well develop into a high-class staying chaser. **Colin Tizzard**

Conclusion: *Smart staying novice chaser in 2015/16, second in 4-miler at Cheltenham before winning the Grade 1 Mildmay Novices' at Aintree, and bound to win more big races; has a lazy streak but improved for fitting of cheekpieces on final two starts and unbeaten in three outings when making the running*

Oceane (Fr) h129p

4 b.g. Kentucky Dynamite (USA) – Zahrana (Fr) (Zamindar (USA))
2015/16 h17.7g* h16g* h16.4d⁴ h16g⁴ h15.7d² Sep 17(F)

Oceane will have gone into last season on a few people's radars as a juvenile hurdler to watch out for based largely on one piece of Flat form: his first run for Alan King (after coming from France) when he finished a close third in a three-year-old handicap at Salisbury. The two horses in front of Oceane that day were Simple Verse and Polarisation who'd go on to much better things in 2015, with the former winning the St Leger and the Champions Fillies' And Mares' Stakes and the latter landing the Melrose Handicap and the Lanark Silver Bell. Though Oceane didn't build on that run straight away in two subsequent Flat starts, he did make a stylish start to his hurdling career when winning at Fontwell last October and at Kempton later that month. Oceane couldn't quite cut it in graded company on his next two outings but he bounced back to a large extent when runner-up to Adrien du Pont making his handicap hurdle debut (off 132) at Ascot in April. What really makes Oceane interesting for this jumps campaign, however, is his progress on the level over the summer. While cheekpieces didn't do much for Oceane first time at York in June, they've certainly benefited since as he's won a mile-and-three-quarter handicap back at Ascot, finished a very eye-catching third in the Goodwood Stakes and quickly got back to winning ways in a two-mile handicap back at York. Oceane was only mid-field when favourite for the Cesarewitch Trial at Newmarket last time, but that might have been once race too many for the time being and, hopefully, he'll have a break before he resumes over hurdles. Oceane's most recent win came off a mark of 87, which suggests he should still be fairly treated off his new hurdles mark of 134, while the step up beyond two miles should suit over timber considering he's proven himself over twenty-one furlongs on the Flat. His best efforts have come on a sound surface. ***Alan King***

Conclusion: *Won twice from five starts as a juvenile hurdler last term and his progress on the Flat this summer suggests he's still well handicapped from a mark of 134, especially with his stamina still to explore over timber*

Otago Trail (Ire) c142

8 b.g. Heron Island (Ire) – Cool Chic (Ire) (Roselier (Fr))
2015/16 c17.5s² c19.2v* c19.4v* c19.9v³ c25dᵖᵘ c20.5d³ Apr 16

The Cheltenham Festival has become so colossal in the way it towers over the rest of the jumps season that the trade paper had a front page dedicated to the 2017 Gold Cup in early-September, over five months before the race was scheduled to take place. What's more, it was just a few days before the Sprint Cup at Haydock. Not all National Hunt trainers gear everything around Cheltenham, however.

Otago Trail sluices through the mud to win at Chepstow

It would certainly be wrong to expect to see Otago Trail at the Festival next spring; not unless the course's famed drainage system suffers a chronic failure, or it teems down Biblical style for days on end just prior to the meeting. Because all the evidence so far suggests Otago Trail is best in the mud. Probably deep mud, too. But that doesn't mean he won't be a horse to have on side this winter, as there's always plenty of testing ground around at some stage; it's just a question of showing patience and waiting for the right conditions. That's something Venetia Williams is very good at. She knows it's not all about Cheltenham, and very few trainers in recent years have been better at targeting big weekend pots through the heart of the jumps season proper.

The further the going stick sinks in, the better we expect Otago Trail to fare in good handicap chases. Forget the fact that his 2015/16 campaign ended with a whimper—there were valid excuses for all three flops after a couple of wins (useful form) under big weights in handicaps at Exeter and Chepstow—and expect him to return well-schooled and with his confidence restored. His trainer will doubtless have already identified some suitable target, so all we need now is for the Gulf Stream and, more specifically the North Atlantic Drift, to do its thing. *Venetia Williams*

Conclusion: *Probably a smart handicap chaser in the making under the right conditions, specifically 2½m on testing ground*

Our Kaempfer (Ire) ★ h143p

7 b.g. Oscar (Ire) – Gra-Bri (Ire) (Rashar (USA))
2015/16 h19.5g⁴ h24.7s² h22.8vᵇᵈ h24g⁵ Mar 17

Our Kaempfer ('warrior' in German) could manage only third on his sole run in points, but he made an immediate impact under Rules when winning a Worcester bumper in 2013 and has since proven himself a useful hurdler, marginally better than his full brother Clondaw Kaempfer thanks to novice wins at Market Rasen and Kempton in early-2015 and several other performances. Our Kaempfer actually came third to Thistlecrack in the Grade 1 Sefton Novices' Hurdle at Aintree, and he produced three efforts in handicaps which were just as good last term, namely when fourth in the Silver Trophy at Chepstow on his return, second to Broxbourne at Aintree and fifth in the Pertemps Final at Cheltenham. Our Kaempfer was perhaps unlucky not to go close on more than one of those occasions too, as he was hindered by a tactical race at Aintree and was ridden with exaggerated waiting tactics at the Festival. Our Kaempfer was also in the process of running well when brought down five out in the Betfair "Fixed Brush" Handicap at Haydock on his penultimate start.

Though he has unfinished business over hurdles, the tall Our Kaempfer has the size to make an even better chaser. The one negative with his prospects for small-field novice chases is the fact he's usually ridden with plenty of restraint, which could leave him vulnerable, but the flip side of that is he should be suited by the return to bigger fields when it comes to contesting handicap chases, especially at the big spring meetings.
Charlie Longsdon

Conclusion: *Hold-up performer who remains with potential over hurdles but is really seen as a staying chaser; likely to win a novice or two but may really thrive in big-field handicaps*

Adam Brookes, Features Writer (Our Kaempfer): *"Our Kaempfer has had a fairly successful career over hurdles so far, winning twice and finishing in the frame in some good handicaps, but it could get even better should he switch to chasing this season. Our Kaempfer took well to Haydock's over-sized hurdles before being brought down last November and certainly has the physical scope to jump the larger obstacles, whilst he hails from the yard that has done well in chases with the likes of Killala Quay, Pendra and Pete The Feat."*

 Follow us on Twitter @Timeform

Out Sam

c141p

7 b.g. Multiplex – Tintera (Ire) (King's Theatre (Ire))
2015/16 h20d⁶ c21d³ c19.2s* c23.4v* c25g c25d Apr 8

Here's hoping the tenure of the new manager of the England football team isn't as underwhelming as the final two runs for Out Sam were in 2015/16. Out Sam finished well held in both the handicap chase won by fellow novice Un Temps Pour Tout at the Cheltenham Festival and the Grade 1 Manifesto Novices' Chase at Aintree, but he'd previously looked a young chaser going places and is taken to get back on track in the new season.

Out Sam showed useful form in a handful of races over hurdles (the first three for Nicky Henderson in 2014/15) and it didn't take long at all for him to reach the same level over fences. After acquitting himself well when thrown into the deep end for his chasing debut in the Grade 2 Noel Novices' at Ascot in December—he finished third of six to Le Mercury—Out Sam put that experience to good use when winning three-runner novices at Catterick in January and Newbury (by three and a half lengths from subsequent Midlands Grand National runner-up Milansbar) in February. Out Sam was being talked about as a possible RSA Chase contender at the Festival but in the event ran in the Ultima Handicap Chase, where he was sent off at 13/2f. He ultimately still looked in need of experience against seasoned handicappers and finished seventh

Out Sam clears the water on the way to winning at Newbury

of twenty-three. Out Sam was undone by his track position as well, the writing soon on the wall as he found himself behind following a tardy start and some tentative leaps, and it was actually to his credit that he could make up the ground he did in a race dominated by those ridden close to the pace. Even his trainer said after the race: "Out Sam found his inexperience was too much in a hot handicap. He got too far back but stayed on well to finish seventh. The race will not be wasted on him and is sure to help his progression later down the line." Out Sam finished last of the seven finishers behind Native River at Ainree but he'd possibly just gone off the boil, while he was also again asked to run on ground quicker than the testing conditions he'd revelled in at both Catterick and Newbury (his two hurdles wins also came on soft ground). Out Sam stays twenty-three furlongs and remains with potential as a chaser. **Warren Greatrex**

Conclusion: *Matched his useful hurdles form over fences in his first season for his new yard in 2015/16; down the field at Cheltenham and Aintree but had looked promising previously and return to soft ground should suit; stays 23f*

Protek des Flos (Fr)   h133

4 b.g. Protektor (Ger) – Flore de Chantenay (Fr) (Smadoun (Fr))
2015/16 h17.9s² h16.8v* h16v* h17.9s² Mar 27

The Prix Virelan may not be one of the most prestigious jumps races in France, nor one regularly targeted by British and Irish trainers, but it was perhaps no great surprise Protek des Flos contested the latest renewal as the same owner's Urbain de Sivola had been the last British-trained runner in 2012. Protek des Flos lost his perfect record for Nicky Henderson as he was beaten by his chief market rival Saint Goustan Blue, but it was still just about a career best on ratings and he might well have gone for home too early given he'd opened up a four-length lead on the home turn only to be beaten half a length. Protek des Flos has previously looked a young hurdler going places with wins in the Grade 2 Finesse Novices' at Cheltenham (sprang a 25/1 shock on his British debut) and a novice at Sandown, and his potential remains intact, especially for fences given he's a useful-looking half-brother to fairly useful chaser Saint des Flos.

Protek des Flos ran once in the French provinces on the Flat and finished second in a listed event for newcomers at Auteuil on his hurdling debut last September. He was then purchased privately by Potensis Bloodstock Ltd and sent to Henderson, for whom he was the bigger-priced representative in the Finesse behind Consul de Thaix. In the event, Consul de Thaix could finish only third to Protek des Flos, who swooped late to beat fellow *Fifty* member Clan des Obeaux by a length and a quarter. The success was Henderson's third in the race in the past four seasons following Rolling Star (2013) and Peace And Co (2015), and the trainer described the winner as "only a baby". Protek des Flos made the most of a good opportunity at Sandown (received weight from his elders as a juvenile) three weeks later, which saw his odds cut for the Triumph Hurdle to 8/1, though he was declared a non-runner in the weeks leading up to that race. Protek des Flos returned to Auteuil for the Prix Virelan only nine days after the Triumph and lost little in defeat as the winner. Has since won a Grade 3 chase and two listed hurdles. **Nicky Henderson**

Conclusion: *Showed useful form after joining top yard from France last season and can go up another notch this term, whether kept over hurdles or sent chasing; will be suited by 2½m*

Romain de Senam (Fr) ★   h138

4 b.g. Saint des Saints (Fr) – Salvatrixe (Fr) (Housamix (Fr))
2015/16 h15.3g* h16.4d³ h15.7d² h16v⁵ h16.4g² h17s⁵ Apr 7

The list of Paul Nicholls-trained horses who were beaten in the Fred Winter Juvenile Handicap Hurdle at the Cheltenham Festival makes for very interesting reading. The race was first run in 2005 and has been won by Nicholls with Sanctuaire in 2010, Qualando in 2015 and Diego du Charmil in 2016, but the list of vanquished horses includes Ptit Zig, Saphir du Rheu and All Yours (as well as Bouvreuil who is another of this season's *Fifty*). Romain de Senam was actually unlucky not to win the latest Fred Winter, despite starting at 20/1, as he still had eleven horses in front of him turning

Romain de Senam just fails to pip his stablemate Diego du Charmil in the Fred Winter

for home and was beaten only a head, and he should be the latest to uphold the positive record.

Romain de Senam wasn't in the same form at Aintree three weeks after Cheltenham, finishing a well-beaten fifth of nine to very impressive winner Apple's Jade in the Grade 1 Anniversary 4-Y-O Hurdle, and he'd also been beaten on his three starts leading up to the Festival (including at 4/1-on). However, we still feel he has more to offer. That could even come over fences this season as he shares his sire with Djakadam and Quito de La Roque— as well as Irish Saint whom Nicholls saddled to win three novices chases (including the Grade 2 Pendil) last term—and is out of a winning chaser, as well as being a half-brother to another in Santa Senam. Santa Senam won over two and a half miles, but Romain de Senam may prove best at the minimum trip for the time being as he's a strong traveller who has worn a hood on his last four starts (also had a tongue tie applied at Sandown when running poorly); with that in mind, it's probably no coincidence that he ran so well in a big field at the Festival. *Paul Nicholls*

Conclusion: *Had a rather hit-and-miss second half of 2015/16 but was unlucky not to win the Fred Winter Handicap Hurdle; strong traveller (wears hood) and may be best suited by big-field scenario over 2m*

Seeyouatmidnight $\quad$ c153
8 b.g. Midnight Legend – Morsky Baloo (Morpeth)
2015/16 c20v³ c23.4v* c20.8v* c23.4s* c24.4g c31.8d³ Apr 16

The latest RSA Chase was one for the smaller guys, so to speak, as horses from the powerhouse yards of Mullins, Nicholls, Henderson, Elliott and O'Neill and owned by such as Graham and Andrea Wylie, J.P. McManus, Gigginstown Stud and Simon Munir and Isaac Souede all came unstuck behind the Sarah Such and Gino Paletta-owned Blaklion from the Nigel Twiston-Davies stable. Such has been a rather lucky owner as her colours are also carried by The New One, and so has Quona Thomson whose Seeyouatmidnight (trained by her husband Sandy Thomson) has won six races and also contested the latest RSA.

Seeyouatmidnight was a Grade 2 winner over hurdles, and he matched that feat over fences last season, when his success in the Dipper Novices' at Cheltenham was book-ended by wins in regulation novices at Kelso and Newcastle. Seeyouamidnight actually beat Blaklion in the Dipper, albeit receiving 3 lb from that rival, and he started fourth best in the market for the RSA at 9/1, despite having openly suffered an interrupted preparation. It could have been the lack of a smooth lead-up to the race that did for Seeyouamidnight at Cheltenham (where he finished seventh of eight) but the good ground was also the quickest he'd ever encountered. Seeyouatmidnight got right back on track on good to soft going when just over two and three-quarter

Seeyouatmidnight beats Blaklion in the Dipper at Cheltenham

lengths third of twenty-eight to Vicente in the Scottish Grand National at Ayr a month later, producing his best ever effort and headed only at the final fence when making a mistake (might have even finished second without that error). Seeyouatmidnight proved he stays four miles at Ayr and looks set to be a big player in all the big long-distance handicap chases this season, with the Welsh National perhaps at the top of his agenda given his form figures on soft/heavy ground read 1123112. **Sandy Thomson**

Conclusion: *Won three times as a novice chaser last term and signed off with good third in Scottish Grand National; looks a player for all the valuable long-distance handicap chases provided the ground is suitable (goes well on softer than good)*

Sharpasaknife (Ire) h128

6 b.g. Flemensfirth (USA) – Omas Lady (Ire) (Be My Native (USA))
2015/16 h19.7v* h20.6v² h18.9g* h20.2g⁴ Apr 21

The Cheltenham Festival has been accused in some quarters of providing an increasingly overbearing presence during each National Hunt season, something touched upon in the entry on Otago Trail in this book. What cannot be questioned is how difficult it is to win any race at the meeting, especially one of the handicaps which always feature big fields, so when Malcolm Jefferson saddled Cape Tribulation and Attaglance to win the Pertemps Final and Martin Pipe Conditionals' Hurdle respectively at the 2012 Festival, before both followed up from revised marks at Aintree's Grand National fixture, it has to be seen as a fantastic training performance.

Sharpasaknife is only just starting out on the road trodden by that pair, but the early signs are very positive as he won two of his four starts over hurdles in his first season in 2015/16. Sharpasaknife had a next-time-out winner in second when he made a winning debut in a novice at Wetherby in January and he had another back in third when getting back to winning ways on his handicap debut (heavily backed for a novice event) over the "fixed brush" hurdles at Haydock in March. In fact, that Haydock form looks especially strong now as the three horses that finished immediately behind Sharpasaknife went on to win nine races between them by mid-August. Sharpasaknife wasn't in the same form in an open handicap at Perth on his final start, jumping poorly back over conventional obstacles, but we already know he's much better than that and is worth another chance.

It may not be too long before Sharpasaknife is sent over fences, and he's certainly a chaser on looks, though there will be plenty of opportunities for him to develop further over timber if connections choose. Given his success at Haydock it could even be that the Betfair "Fixed Brush" Handicap Hurdle there in November may be the race for him, especially as the Jefferson yard won it with According To Pete in 2008. *Malcolm Jefferson*

Conclusion: *Went a fair way in a short space of time in 2015/16 and taken to bounce back from a low-key final start; chasing type who could be one for the Betfair "Fixed Brush" Handicap Hurdle at Haydock given he's already won there*

 ## Tomngerry (Ire)   h136
6 b.g. Craigsteel – Lady Vic (Ire) (Old Vic)
2015/16 b16.8v* b15.7v* h21.3v* h22s* h24.7d^pu Apr 8

We don't know whether Tomngerry is named after the cartoon adversaries created by Hanna-Barbera in the 1940s or two of the main characters in the 1970s BBC sitcom about a couple keen to avoid the rat race by becoming self-sufficient—or maybe neither given the spelling. But we do feel the gelding has the potential to provide us with a bit of The Good Life in the coming months and, in the age-old battle of punters versus bookmakers, hopefully he'll have the former group looking like the cat who caught the mouse on several occasions.

Tomngerry has an impressive strike rate so far, unbeaten in a point and two bumpers and two from three over hurdles, with his only defeat coming when stepped up in grade and seemingly not himself when pulled up in the Grade 1 Sefton Novices' Hurdle at Aintree. Prior to that, however, he'd looked a really good staying prospect, one who clearly handles deep ground well and has both an enthusiastic way of going about things and plenty of stamina. Presumably, Tomngerry will start off in staying handicap hurdles this winter and he's another (like Sharpasaknife) who could have the

Betfair "Fixed Brush" Handicap at Haydock on his agenda in the first instance, a race the Brian Ellison stable targeted with a similar type in Definitly Red (found only Baradari too good) last year. Like Definitly Red, Tomngerry probably won't be long before going chasing if connections feel there aren't more races to be won with him as a hurdler, and chances are he'll prove at least as good in that sphere, too. **Brian Ellison**

Conclusion: *Has won all four of his completed starts (including two over hurdles before being pulled up in the Sefton at Aintree) and remains relatively unexposed; can pick up a valuable staying handicap hurdle before going chasing*

Simon Walker, Head of Editorial (Tomngerry): *"The number of good jumpers trained in the North has been on the wane for a good number of years now, but Brian Ellison is doing his best to keep the flag flying for that part of Britain and, in Tomngerry, he's got one that is bound to win more races if sensibly campaigned, staying handicap hurdles surely first on the agenda followed by novice chasing if and when the handicapper gets his measure."*

Two Taffs (Ire)   h135p

6 b.g. Flemensfirth (USA) – Richs Mermaid (Ire) (Saddlers' Hall (Ire))
2015/16 h16.7g³ h16d² h16d³ h19.8s⁴ h21.4d* Apr 16

It was Two Taffs' victory in a handicap hurdle on Scottish Grand National Day at Ayr which brought up the seasonal century for Dan Skelton, and the six-year-old looks the type to provide more success for the trainer in the new season.

After making a winning debut in a Market Rasen bumper in March 2015, Two Taffs failed to get his head in front in his first four starts over hurdles last term, though he improved with each run, finishing fourth of eighteen to Barney Dwan in a typically well-contested final of the EBF 'National Hunt' Novices' Hurdle series at Sandown in March after ten weeks off. Two Taffs wasn't seen to best advantage in that race either, as he was forced to deliver his challenge from further back than ideal and suffered interference just as he was beginning to move into contention. He gained a deserved first success over timber back in an open handicap at Ayr in April, stepped up to an extended twenty-one furlongs as he beat fellow improver Missed Approach by three lengths. Two Taffs still didn't look the finished article once hitting the front and he should have plenty of progress left in him, certainly enough to overcome his new mark of 138 (raised 9 lb). Indeed, Two Taffs—whose part-owner Dai Walters has secured the services of top Irish rider Davy Russell for this season—has the makings of a smart hurdler and can be expected to play a leading role in some of the biggest handicaps. *Dan Skelton*

Conclusion: *Well-made gelding who will make a chaser but still looks well treated over hurdles; strong traveller but proved he stays 21f last term and one to follow in handicaps around that trip*

Vintage Clouds (Ire)   h132

6 gr.g. Cloudings (Ire) – Rare Vintage (Ire) (Germany (USA))
2015/16 h20d² h18.9v* h15.7v² h18.9v² h22.8v² h24.7d^pu Apr 8

Without wanting to delve into the racing cliché book when assessing Vintage Clouds' career so far, there's no doubt that 'the bigger picture' must be considered. Vintage Clouds failed to improve upon the useful form he showed when winning a novice over the "fixed brush" hurdles at Haydock last November on his second start over timber, beaten at short odds there on his next two outings, but there's a strong chance that the plan has always been chasing and the foundations he laid last season should be used to good effect this time around.

It's not as if Vintage Clouds' form regressed in 2015/16, either. His three lengths second to Jonniesofa (who received 3 lb) in the Grade 2 Prestige Novices' Hurdle, again at Haydock, in February was probably as good as his earlier nine-length defeat of Baratineur. Vintage Clouds appeared to appreciate the step up to two and three-quarter miles on that occasion and went over the extended three miles in the Grade 1 Sefton Novices' at Aintree (20/1) subsequently, though he couldn't reproduce his best form away from testing ground and Haydock's specialist obstacles, eventually being pulled up. Vintage Clouds is certainly worth another try at three miles (his half-brother Vintage Star stays further) and he also looks on a fair opening mark of 137 for handicap hurdles, though chasing is hopefully the plan this season. It would be no great surprise to see him follow a similar path to Vintage Star and the same owner's Many Clouds whose novice chase campaigns both included a crack at the RSA Chase at the Cheltenham Festival (before contesting the Grand National the following year, the latter winning the Aintree spectacular, of course). *Sue Smith*

Conclusion: *Useful hurdler who will make a chaser; could even develop into an RSA contender*

Westend Story (Ire) ★   b116p

5 b.g. Westerner – Sarahall (Ire) (Saddlers' Hall (Ire))
2015/16 b15.8s* b16.8v* b16.4g^5 Mar 16

It almost has the makings of a West End story, though the script for the final scenes hasn't been written yet. During a career as a jockey that saw him win the Grand National on Rough Quest in 1996 and Cheltenham Gold Cup on See More Business in 1999, as well as become the leading jockey at the Cheltenham Festival in 1999 and 2000, Mick Fitzgerald has in recent years turned his attention to broadcasting. After initially working for At The Races, Fitzgerald joined Channel 4 Racing in 2013 and it was announced this August that he had been signed up to join the newly-assembled presenting team for ITV, who will be racing's terrestrial broadcaster from 2017. Oh, and the Mick Fitzgerald Racing Club-owned Westend Story is one of the most interesting novice hurdling prospects around for the new jumps season.

Westend Story struggled to uphold his family's tradition in points—his dam Sarahall won between the flags, as did his full brother Wild Bill—as he fell on both his starts in Ireland, but he made a winning debut for Philip Hobbs in a bumper at Huntingdon on Boxing Day. It was a six-length win too, with the rest strung out behind, and Westend Story tripled that margin of success under a penalty in a five-runner similar race at Exeter in mid-February. The fact that Westend Story's two impressive wins had come under testing conditions was only a footnote, as he'd travelled extremely smoothly on both occasions, and he produced an even better performance on good ground in the Champion Bumper at Cheltenham, finishing three and a quarter lengths fifth of twenty-three to Ballyandy but unlucky not to go closer having met some trouble on the home turn before finishing with a flourish. The lengthy Westend Story is a future chaser, but he'll have his say in some top novice hurdles first. He'll prove suited by further than two miles. ***Philip Hobbs***

Conclusion: *Showed smart form in bumpers last season, winning twice before looking unlucky not to finish closer than fifth in the Champion Bumper; can prove a leading novice hurdler in 2016/17*

Whataknight   h142

7 b.g. Midnight Legend – What A Mover (Jupiter Island)
2015/16 h21.4v^3 h23.9s* h24.4d^2 h23.1v^3 h20.3g^4 :: 2016/17 h22.8m* May 7

Question: Which horse did amateur jockey Will Biddick ride to five successive wins in 2014/15? Answer: Whataknight. Those victories may only have been in points, but they provided Harry Fry's charge with a very solid foundation on which to begin his career under Rules. Whataknight showed plenty to work on under considerate handling when third in a Wincanton novice on his hurdling debut last November, and he got off the mark stepped up to three miles at Taunton the following month from a next-time-out winner. Whataknight was then beaten on his handicap debut at Doncaster two months later, but he went like the best horse at the weights for a long way before being pipped by fellow *Fifty* member Emerging Force, with another seventeen horses sixteen lengths and more behind them. Whataknight was turned over at odds-on back in novice company at Exeter on his next start, though he perhaps needed longer to get over his previous run twenty-six days earlier, while he appeared to find the drop to two and a half miles against him at Cheltenham in April. Whataknight's two low-key efforts saw him start at 12/1 for his second handicap at Haydock in May and he overcame those odds in style, travelling smoothly and staying on strongly to score by five lengths from Minella Daddy in a field of fifteen. Though a 6 lb rise (to 144) still leaves Whataknight looking favourably-treated, he will reportedly go chasing this autumn, which should suit him very well. Whataknight's wins have come on soft and good to firm ground, which opens up the options for his connections this season, and he looks sure to win novice chases for his excellent trainer; indeed, the fact he's an uncomplicated ride who travels strongly should be to his advantage in such races which often feature small fields. **Harry Fry**

Conclusion: *Showed form bordering on smart as a hurdler in his first season and looks a good prospect for staying novice chases; has won on soft and good to firm ground*

Who Dares Wins (Ire)   h135
4 b.g. Jeremy (USA) – Savignano (Polish Precedent (USA))
2015/16 h15.8d* h16.6v* h16.8v⁴ h16.8g Sep 16 (F)

We're taking a bit of a chance including both Oceane and Who Dares Wins in this season's *Fifty* as former jumpers who have done well on the Flat over the summer don't always return to the winter game as you'd expect. They are both in the same yard too, but Who Dares Wins is undoubtedly another gelding who'll look very well handicapped if sent back over timber.

Both horses were juvenile hurdlers last term and have since shown improved form back on the level, with Who Dares Wins picking up from where he left off with Richard Hannon in 2015 (won three handicaps) when winning a twelve-furlong handicap at Chester in late-July. That effort came on Who Dares Wins' first start since finishing well held in the Triumph Hurdle at the Cheltenham Festival in March and saw him beat progressive three-year-old Against The Odds by five lengths. Who Dares Wins has not been quite so good in similar races since, back up to a mile and three-quarters (had won over that trip previously) when third at Nottingham twelve days later and back over twelve furlongs when three lengths last of five at Newbury, but he was just unable to claw back a pair that were better placed the way things went on the first occasion and then probably should have gone harder in front on the second. Going back to Who Dares Wins' career as a hurdler, the fact he was sent off at 10/1 for the Triumph shows that he hasn't done too badly in that sphere, either. Who Dares Wins made a successful jumping debut at Ludlow last November before following up in the Grade 2 Summit Juvenile at Doncaster by twenty lengths. Who Dares Wins matched his Doncaster form when fourth behind two other Fifty members, Protek des Flos and Clan des Obeax, at Cheltenham next time, with his performance worth marking up after he pressed on too soon with the latter. Like Oceane, Who Dares Wins still has his stamina to explore over hurdles, and he too can win a good-quality handicap from a mark of 139. *Alan King*

Conclusion: *Has a similar profile to the same stable's Oceane having improved returned to the Flat this summer and still with his stamina to explore over hurdles*

Winter Escape (Ire) ★   h142P

5 b.g. Robin des Pres (Fr) – Saddleeruppat (Ire) (Saddlers' Hall (Ire))
2015/16 h16.6d* h16.6d* h16g* Feb 27

We included an unbeaten, J. P. McManus-owned hurdler with a Large 'P' attached to his Timeform rating is this publication last year and, after a slow start to the campaign, Minella Rocco went on to win at the Cheltenham Festival. Hopefully, Winter Escape can provide similar success. He's certainly looked a highly exciting young hurdler in three starts so far and could be one for the very valuable Betfair Hurdle at Newbury in February.

Winter Escape was strong in the betting (15/8f) ahead of his debut in a big-field maiden hurdle at Doncaster in December and he justified the support with plenty in hand. So impressive was Winter Escape that he was sent off at 5/1-on to shrug off a penalty in a novice at the same track two months later, and he landed those odds in equally impressive fashion, again tanking through the race before hitting the line with six lengths to spare over runner-up Bantam. Winter Escape was finally forced off the bridle as he extended his unbeaten record in the five-runner Grade 2 Dovecote Novices' Hurdle at Kempton later in February, yet the feeling left was still most positive given the run of the race was against him, with the sprint finish not ideal for one so inexperienced. The 6/4-on favourite Winter Escape came under pressure as the well-ridden Marracudja quickened in the straight, not helped by edging right through greenness after two out and jumping left at the last, but his ability shone through by the end as he scored by a length and a quarter from that rival. Once Winter Escape was straightened out on the flat he forged to the front without firm pressure, with the body language of his rider Barry Geraghty leaving the impression he always felt

Winter Escape jumps to the front in the Dovecote at Kempton

he had the runner-up covered. It was soon announced that Winter Escape would skip the Cheltenham Festival and wait for Aintree, though he didn't run there either and reportedly went back to his owner's stud in Ireland for the summer.

Winter Escape cost €52,000 as a three-year-old and already looks a good purchase. As a half-brother to the fairly useful hurdles winner at up to two and a quarter miles Lughnasa (by Westerner) out of a close relative to the high-class staying hurdler Black Jack Ketchum and the useful hurdler at up to three miles Apache Jack, it might be expected that Winter Escape will stay further than two miles. However, he possesses lots of natural speed and certainly doesn't need a step up in distance yet. He's raced only on good or good to soft ground. **Alan King**

Conclusion: *Highly progressive in winning his three starts in 2015/16, including the Grade 2 Dovecote Novices' Hurdle at Kempton; looks the type to land a good prize in the new season, possibly the Betfair Hurdle in February*

Wolf Sword (Ire) c114

7 b.g. Flemensfirth (USA) – Dame O'Neill (Ire) (Dr Massini (Ire))
2015/16 h19.5d* h19.7g⁵ c16.5dᵖᵘ c15.7s⁵ c20.5v⁵ c21.3dᶠ c21.3s² :: 2016/17
c20m² May 5

Whilst no disrespect is meant toward George Moore, the ears of a few at Timeform pricked up when they heard that Wolf Sword had joined Sue Smith upon his former trainer's retirement in January. A bumper and hurdles winner for Moore—who saddled nine winners in 2015/16 at a strike-rate of 10%—Wolf Sword had also showed signs he was beginning to click as a chaser prior to joining Smith. Having trained Aurora's Encore to land the 2013 Grand National, as well as a record three individual winners of the Grade 2 Peter Marsh Chase (including Cloudy Too last term), Smith's skill with chasers is well known, and she instantly found the key to Wolf Sword. Wolf Sword was backed into 5/4 when making his debut for Smith in a handicap chase at Wetherby in March and was in the process of showing improved form when he fell at the last. Our honest reflection is that Wolf Sword would have finished second had he stood up, having perhaps done a bit too much too soon, and he filled the runner-up spot in similar races at the same track and at Carlisle on his next two outings, but we feel there are still several races to be won with him by his new yard. The form of those second-place finishes has stacked up well too, as he was beaten by the subsequent winner of Perth's Highland National, Double Whammy, on the first occasion and then by novice What Happens, who also won his next two starts, on the second. Wolf Sword stays twenty-one furlongs, acts on soft and good to firm going and often races prominently (strong traveller). **Sue Smith**

Conclusion: *Improved after joining Sue Smith early in the year, finishing second to subsequent winners at both Wetherby and Carlisle; can win handicap chases at around 21f in the North*

Wotzizname (Ire) h138p

6 b.g. Fruits of Love (USA) – Native Bean (Ire) (Be My Native (USA))
2015/16 h23.1d* :: 2016/17 h23.3d* May 5

Given his subsequent exploits under Rules, it's hard to fathom how it took five attempts for Wotzizname to get off the mark in points, and even after that success he was beaten twice more between the flags. Wotzizname's lack of winning prowess in the amateur game might well have contributed to him being sent off at 9/1 for his hurdling debut in a twelve-runner event at Exeter in April, but he hammered his rivals by fifteen lengths and upwards (the front two in the market following him home) and looked a young horse to keep firmly on side. The impression was cemented when Wotzizname followed up under a penalty at Uttoxeter the following month in equally impressive fashion. Both wins were recorded at close to three miles, though the way Wotzizname travelled (on good to soft ground) suggests he won't have a problem dropping back in trip if his connections wish. The combination of the fact that Wotzizname will lose his novice status in early-November and his owner Charles Horton (for whom Wotzizname was a first winner when scoring in that point at Larkhill) is reportedly a chasing enthusiast may mean that the gelding is sent over fences sooner rather than later, but that doesn't worry us as he should prove an exciting prospect over the larger obstacles based on what we've seen to date…under Rules, at least. **Harry Fry**

Conclusion: *Won just one of his seven starts in points but has looked a smart prospect in winning both his starts over hurdles and can do damage from an opening mark of 140; will also make a chaser; stays 23f*

SECTION

Apple's Jade comes home miles clear in the Anniversary 4-Y-O Hurdle at Aintree

Apple's Jade (Fr)   h157p

4 b.f. Saddler Maker (Ire) – Apple's For Ever (Fr) (Nikos)
2015/16 h16.4d* h16v* h16.8g² h17s* :: 2016/17 h16d* Apr 30

Defeat in the Triumph Hurdle as a four-year-old doesn't necessarily prevent a horse from becoming a top-notch performer later on in its career. For example, the highest-rated hurdler in Timeform history, Night Nurse, could manage only tenth in the 1975 Triumph (admittedly staged on barely raceable ground) but then went unbeaten through his next ten starts, including a smooth all-the-way success in the 1976 Champion Hurdle—he repeated the feat in a vintage renewal of hurdling's blue riband twelve months later, when chased home by Monksfield (himself a future dual Champion Hurdle winner) who had finished runner-up in the 1976 Triumph. Another multiple champion hurdler, See You Then (successful in 1985, 1986 and 1987), had filled the runner-up spot when a hot favourite for the 1984 Triumph. It may be too soon to mention Apple's Jade in the same breath as those illustrious horses, but if there was one member of last season's crop of juveniles who is likely to emerge as a live 2017 Champion Hurdle contender then it's surely her, even though she was only head bridesmaid behind Ivanovich Gorbatov in the Triumph.

Unraced on the Flat, the ex-French Apple's Jade lacked the experience of most her rivals when lining up in a fifteen-runner Triumph Hurdle on what was just her third career start (and only her second for current connections). Despite losing her unbeaten record, Apple's Jade still announced herself as an above-average juvenile as she went down by just a length and a quarter to the well-backed favourite, pulling clear of the remainder. It didn't take long for Apple's Jade to prove herself better than Ivanovich Gorbatov, however, reversing the placings with that rival when recording hugely impressive Grade 1 wins at Aintree (by forty-one lengths) and Punchestown on her subsequent starts. Apple's Jade looked a star in the making both times. Though she will stay further than two miles in due course, Apple's Jade clearly has plenty of speed and it seems logical that she'll be aimed at the Champion Hurdle initially, with the Mares' Hurdle there as a back-up option if it's needed. Both her physique (tall and unfurnished) and upwardly-mobile record to date suggests that further improvement will be forthcoming from Apple's Jade and she already appeals as a serious challenger to her stable's other two star mares, Annie Power and Vroum Vroum Mag, let alone the geldings who will have to concede weight to her. **Willie Mullins**

Conclusion: *Has won four of her five starts over hurdles, including Grade 1 juveniles at Aintree (by a staggering 41 lengths) and Punchestown; could well develop into a live contender for the 2017 Champion Hurdle*

 ## Alisier d'Irlande (Fr) c151+

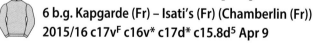

6 b.g. Kapgarde (Fr) – Isati's (Fr) (Chamberlin (Fr))
2015/16 c17v^F c16v* c17d* c15.8d^5 Apr 9

Henry de Bromhead was dealt a significant blow this autumn when it was announced his leading patrons, Alan and Ann Potts, had removed their horses from his yard. The phlegmatic trainer wished his former owners "the best of luck" with their horses, before adding: "We still have a lot of nice horses to look forward to for this season." It is safe to assume Alisier d'Irlande figures prominently in that group and, ironically, the six-year-old is only based in Ireland due to a stable switch in the opposite direction—de Bromhead has been the chief beneficiary of big-spending owner Roger Brookhouse's decision to relocate many of his horses from the powerful West Country yards of Philip Hobbs, David Pipe and Paul Nicholls.

High hopes have been entertained for Alisier d'Irlande ever since he ran out an impressive winner of a four-year-old maiden point on his debut, which prompted

Brookhouse to shell out £300,000 for him less than three weeks later. A stable switch followed defeats on his first two starts over hurdles (for Hobbs) and Alisier d'Irlande has barely looked back since, running out a twenty-one length winner of a maiden hurdle at Thurles on his debut for de Bromhead. It is as a chaser, however, that this strong-travelling sort has really come into his own. An uncharacteristic jumping error (fell four out) robbed him of another wide-margin win on his chasing debut in a Fairyhouse maiden in January, but Alisier d'Irlande made no mistake when easily winning at Naas (by seventeen lengths from useful hurdler Never Enough Time) and Leopardstown on his next two starts in February. Admittedly, Alisier d'Ireland ended up finishing a well-held last of five behind Douvan when upped to Grade 1 company on his final start, but he did pay a big price for trying to mix things with that outstanding rival and actually remained on the bridle for much longer than others who tried to do the same last season. Provided he can steer clear of Douvan, there should be plenty of good races to be won by Alisier d'Irlande in 2016/17 and he could even develop into a top-class two-mile chaser like his stable-companion Special Tiara. **Henry de Bromhead**

Conclusion: *Looked a potentially very smart 2m chaser when winning twice last season and should win good races this term provided he can steer clear of Douvan; strong-travelling front runner*

 ## Anibale Fly (Fr)   h145p

6 b.g. Assessor (Ire) – Nouba Fly (Fr) (Chamberlin (Fr))
2015/16 h16v* h20v³ h16d⁴ h16s⁶ :: 2016/17 h20d* Apr 30

County Meath trainer Tony Martin has excelled at plundering valuable handicaps both over jumps and on the Flat, and he landed one of the most famous gambles this century when Xenophon justified favouritism in the 2003 County Hurdle under Mick Fitzgerald. However, a first Grade 1 victory did not come Martin's way until Bog Warrior took the Drinmore Novices' Chase at Fairyhouse in December 2011 and there hasn't been any more since Benefficient won the last of his three Grade 1s in 2013. Martin could lack firepower at the top level again in 2016/17 season with Gigginstown House Stud (who owned Bog Warrior) removing their horses from his yard in May, but the trainer put that blow behind him the following month when winning the very valuable Coral Handicap Hurdle at Punchestown with the J. P. Mcmanus-owned Anibale Fly, who can provide his connections further big-race success this term.

Anibale Fly won two of his three starts in bumpers and confirmed the promise of those efforts when making a winning hurdling debut at Navan last December, when ridden by a professional—Barry Geraghty—for the first time. Anibale Fly still didn't look the finished article when third of four finishers to Bellshill in the Grade 1 Lawlor's Hotel Novices' at Naas next time, and he showed the benefit of that experience when an improved length-and-a-half fourth (next-time-out winners in first and second) making his handicap debut at Leopardstown in February. While stepping up in trip hadn't worked instantly in the Lawlor's Hotel, Anibale Fly looked ready for another go over that distance when sixth of fifteen over two miles at Fairyhouse next time, and he duly got right back on track in the Coral Handicap Hurdle. An 11 lb rise in his hurdles mark (to 146) shouldn't prevent Anibale Fly from winning again, while he also has plenty of scope to make a chaser—whichever route he goes he's a jumper to keep firmly on side this season. *Tony Martin*

Conclusion: *Already smart after five starts over hurdles, winning fiercely competitive renewal of valuable 2½m handicap at Punchestown on final start, and capable of even better; will make a chaser, too*

 Forge Meadow (Ire) b104p

4 b.f. Beneficial – Ballys Baby (Ire) (Bob Back (USA))
2015/16 b16s* :: 2016/17 b16d² Apr 27

The Tattersalls Ireland Sales Bumper at Fairyhouse's Easter Festival is a valuable contest for four- and five-year-olds that have passed through the sales-ring at Tattersalls, and it's often a fairly strong event of its type with several big yards represented. The 2014 renewal will always be remembered for the great bit of business done by Michael Ronayne, who'd picked up the winner Moon Racer for just €5,000 several months before. Moon Racer's seven-and-a-half-length win netted the gelding's owner-trainer Ronayne just shy of €50,000, while an even bigger windfall was to follow when Moon Racer was sold to Professor Caroline Tisdall and Bryan Drew for around five times that amount (when converted into pounds). The form of the 2015 Tattersalls Ireland Sales Bumper also proved reliable, albeit franked belatedly when the winner Castello Sforza finished fourth in last season's Cheltenham Champion Bumper on his next start almost a year later. This year's race looked solid too, as the successful Forge Meadow followed her impressive five-and-a-half-length defeat of Geneva Barracks (in a race contested solely by four-year-olds, sixteen of them) with a three lengths second of fourteen to Augusta Kate in a mares' listed bumper at Punchestown in April. Forge Meadow might not have proved a match for the winner, but she still finished a place in front of Glens Harmony (like Augusta Kate, trained by Willie Mullins and also a full sister to the smart hurdler Glens Melody) who won a fifteen-runner mares' maiden bumper next time by thirteen lengths. Forge Meadow is bred to do the job over jumps being by Beneficial out of a full sister to the useful staying chaser Back On Line (this is the family of Many Clouds) and she looked a good prospect for novice hurdles this season, with the second running of the Dawn Run Mares' Novices' Hurdle at the Cheltenham Festival an obvious big target. *Jessica Harrington*

Conclusion: *Made impressive winning debut in valuable sales bumper and similar form when runner-up to Augusta Kate in listed event; could be one for the Dawn Run Mares' Novices' Hurdle at the Festival*

Gallant Oscar (Ire) c155p

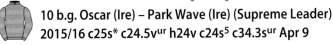

10 b.g. Oscar (Ire) – Park Wave (Ire) (Supreme Leader)
2015/16 c25s* c24.5v^{ur} h24v c24s^5 c34.3s^{ur} Apr 9

Last year's entry on Gallant Oscar began with the phrase "there aren't many nine-year-olds who have a 'p' symbol still attached to their Timeform rating". Well, twelve months and no wins later, it may be surprising to some that the 'p' still adorns the rating of a gelding who is now rising eleven, but we remain convinced we're yet to see the very best of Gallant Oscar. Admittedly, a record of four non-completions from eleven starts over fences is hardly the most convincing record at first glance, but that doesn't tell the whole story—Gallant Oscar doesn't have fundamental jumping issues and he remains one to be interested in valuable staying handicap company. Indeed, he shaped as if well handicapped in such races last season, looking likely to be involved in the shake-up when unseating two out in the Paddy Power Chase at Leopardstown in December and then catching the eye with how strongly he was travelling when parting company with Mark Walsh at the eighteenth in the Grand National in April.

The hurly-burly of large-field events isn't an issue for Gallant Oscar, though, as he showed with a facile success in the 2014 Leinster National at Naas on his first outing outside of novice chase company, whilst his victory in the Pat Taaffe Handicap Chase at the 2015 Punchestown Festival was, if anything, even more impressive—he numbered the subsequent Irish National runner-up Bless The Wings (third) and future Grand National winner Rule The World (sixth) among his victims that day. Given his connections, it wouldn't be a surprise if Gallant Oscar again mixes hurdling with chasing in 2016/17 in order to protect his handicap mark (148) in the latter sphere. Although Gallant Oscar will continue to warrant respect over the smaller obstacles (two wins and three placed efforts from six hurdles starts in past three seasons), it is as a chaser that he earns his inclusion in these pages for the second year running. Hopefully, he'll prove a safer conveyance this time around and, at this stage, he appeals as one of the most interesting contenders for the 2017 Grand National. *Tony Martin*

Conclusion: *Into the veteran stage now but we're still yet to see the very best of him in long-distances chases; like the same owner's Minella Rocco, makes appeal at 33/1 for the Grand National*

 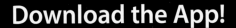

J. P. McManus owns both Gallant Oscar and Great Field

Great Field (Fr)   h147p

5 b.g. Great Pretender (Ire) – Eaton Lass (Ire) (Definite Article)
2015/16 h18d* h16.8g^{pu} Mar 18

What does Great Field have in common with Grade 1 winners Sir des Champs and Apple's Jade? They are obviously all under the care of Willie Mullins—no prizes for that one—but they were also formerly trained in France by Emmanuel Clayeux, whose Saint-Voir-based operation has produced the likes of Aux Ptits Soins, Salut Flo and Une Artiste in recent years, too. More and more of Britain and Ireland's biggest jumps races are being won by horses that began their careers in France, including ten of the twenty-eight races at the 2016 Cheltenham Festival, and Great Field can help continue that trend this time around.

Great Field won two of his three hurdles starts for Clayeux and such was the impression he created when completing the hat-trick in a Leopardstown minor event in February on his first start for Mullins that he was sent off 7/1 joint-favourite for the County Hurdle at the Cheltenham Festival less than three weeks later. Great Field went into the race with a Timeform large 'P' attached to his master rating, which means we felt he was open to significant further improvement, and while it didn't come off that day as he was eventually pulled up, we're still convinced there's lots more to come from him. Simply saying he was pulled up doesn't get anywhere near to the full story with Great Field, either, as he carted his rider Barry Geraghty along in front for most of the way until being headed after two out. Obviously, any repeat of Great Field's free-going antics will make it very difficult for him to win a top-end handicap, but there must be a good chance he'll have learnt from that experience, certainly in the best hands to do so. It should also be pointed out that Great Field's Leopardstown success had come on the back of a sixteen-month break and he's still only five years old. **Willie Mullins**

Conclusion: *Needs to curb his free-going ways but clearly has stacks of natural talent and is also in the best possible hands to learn; can hopefully win a valuable handicap hurdle (stays 2¼m)*

Heartbreak City (Fr) h130p

6 b.g. Lando (Ger) – Moscow Nights (Fr) (Peintre Celebre (USA))
2015/16 h16d* h16.1g* Aug 20(F)

There have been a number of dual-purpose performers from Ireland that have become mainstays in big races in both spheres in recent years, including the Willie Mullins-trained pair of Clondaw Warrior, who won the Ascot Stakes in 2015 and the Galway Plate this season, and Wicklow Brave, who won the County Hurdle in 2015 and sprang a surprise when beating the 7/1-on Order of St George in the Irish St Leger this September. There's also Jarlath Fahey's admirable mare Jennies Jewel, who won the Ascot Stakes at the latest Royal meeting less than six months after chasing home Vroum Vroum Mag in a Grade 2 over hurdles at the same course. Tony Martin is no stranger to high-quality code-switchers, either, with his Quick Jack finishing third in the Ebor before winning a big-field handicap at Leopardstown in September, not much over a year after taking the Galway Hurdle, and Heartbreak City winning twice over hurdles this summer before completing his hat-trick in the aforementioned Ebor at York.

Quick Jack, Wicklow Brave and Clondaw Warrior have all had a crack (or two) at winning what is now Europe's richest flat handicap, but it was Heartbreak City who was able to etch his name on the roll of honour. He did so in a manner rarely seen in the best handicaps too, especially on fast ground, as he beat Shrewd by four lengths under apprentice Adam McNamara; once again Tony Martin was highlighting how shrewd (pardon the pun) he is with using the best young jockeys as Heartbreak City had been ridden to success on his previous starts by Jack Kennedy and Donagh Meyler. Heartbreak City currently has an ITC mark 7 lb higher than when winning off 118 at Galway in July, but he could easily still prove thrown in off his new rating given he defied 103 in style in the Ebor. A successful return to hurdling should see him raised enough to get into some of the big handicaps and he can land one this term for his very good trainer. **Tony Martin**

Conclusion: *Won twice over hurdles this summer but four-length win in the Ebor at York since suggests he'll still be on a very attractive mark should he return to timber; could be one for the big handicaps for his shrewd trainer*

Killer Crow (Ire) c138

7 ch.g. Presenting – Rivervail (Ire) (River Falls)
2015/16 h24d c16d⁴ c19s⁶ c20v c29v⁵ c20v* c19.5v² c21v² c29s c21.1d ::
2016/17 c20d c22.5g h19.5d² c24v^bd Sep 14

At first glance, a record of just one win from twelve starts over fences—plus an average finishing position of twelfth from his last four completed runs in handicap company—hardly screams ideal *Timeform Horse To Follow* material. However, if one digs a little deeper then Killer Crow is (hopefully) a much more interesting horse than his uninspiring recent profile might suggest. Indeed, everything had looked so promising for Killer Crow after the fitting of a tongue strap last winter, wearing the aid for the first time when beating The Winkler (a useful dual winner since) in a two-and-a-half mile novice at Navan for that sole chase success to date. Even better was to come on his next two starts, notably when a never-nearer second to Empire of Dirt (a profitable selection in this book last year) in the valuable Leopardstown Handicap Chase in January.

From the way we read that form, Killer Crow is definitely a well-handicapped horse on that run and arguably capable of better too, considering that he rather conceded first run given how things unfolded. Admittedly things haven't gone to plan for Killer Crow over fences (he was a narrow second in a minor hurdle in August) since then but he's had a number of valid excuses, including when brought down at the fifth in the Kerry National at Listowel (7/1) in mid-September. Killer Crow also failed to stay when seventh in the Irish National (shaped well for a long way) back in March, lost all chance when badly hampered at Becher's in the Topham Chase next time and was then left in an impossible position under a patient ride when down the field in the Galway Plate in July. On a positive note, those unplaced efforts haven't done his handicap mark any harm—132 in Ireland—whilst the fact he is still donning the famous maroon and white Gigginstown silks could be significant. Michael O'Leary is on record saying that he's only interesting in producing graded performers, so the fact that Killer Crow wasn't one of the sizeable annual batch of Gigginstown handicappers heading for the sales this autumn suggests is interesting. Under the excellent care of Gordon Elliott, Killer Crow can be placed to advantage over the coming months. **Gordon Elliott**

Conclusion: *Poor win record over fences doesn't do him justice and can land a good-quality handicap chase this term (brought down early in the Kerry National last time); probably stays 29f and best form on testing ground*

Let's Dance (Fr) h138p

4 b.f. Poliglote – Baraka du Berlais (Fr) (Bonnet Rouge (Fr))
2015/16 h16v² h16v³ h16.8g⁴ :: 2016/17 h16d² h16d* May 23

Let's Dance was making her sixth start over hurdles when getting off the mark in a Sligo maiden in May, but the fact she was sent off at 12/1-on that day should tell plenty of the story when it comes to the form she already had in the book. After one start in France, Let's Dance was turned over at odds-on on her debut for Willie Mullins in a three-year-old maiden at Leopardstown just after Christmas. Hindsight proved she was up against it that day, however, as she bumped into Ivanovich Gorbatov, who would go on to win the Triumph Hurdle in which Let's Dance would take a creditable fourth, six weeks after she'd finished a place ahead of that rival when third to her stablemate Footpad in the Grade 1 Spring Juvenile at Leopardstown. Let's Dance produced her third useful effort on the bounce in another Grade 1 when nine lengths second of five to fellow Irish Horse To Follow Apple's Jade in the AES Champion Four-Year-Old Hurdle at Punchestown, again finishing ahead (and a head) in front of a below-par Ivanovich Gorbatov. Predictably, Let's Dance was one of the easiest winners of the season when cruising home by eight and a half lengths on her final start. Let's Dance presumably takes her name from one of biggest selling tracks by the late David Bowie, so here's hoping she'll have us Dancing In The Street and not feeling Under Pressure, like we're in Quicksand, in the new season. She could have the Dawn Run Mares' Novices' Hurdle or even the David Nicholson Mares' Hurdle at the Cheltenham Festival on her hit list.
Willie Mullins

Conclusion: *In the frame in three Grade 1 juvenile contests before easily winning in maiden company on her final start last term; remains with potential and should make her mark against her own sex this season*

Yorkhill (Ire) h163p

6 ch.g. Presenting – Lightning Breeze (Ire) (Saddlers' Hall (Ire))
2015/16 b16g* h20v* h16v* h21.1g* h20s* :: 2016/17 h16d⁴ Apr 26

In the last couple of years the Festivals at Cheltenham and Aintree have been fairly happy hunting grounds for punters prepared to take short prices, but it quickly became apparent that things were going to be different when the third of the big spring meetings in 2016 rolled around. Yorkhill could manage only fourth behind 16/1-shot Don't Touch It when sent off 9/4-on favourite for the Grade 1 Herald

Champion Novices' Hurdle at Punchestown in late-April, but everything that Yorkhill had done prior strongly suggests that a line can be safely put through his run and he remains a top-class performer in the making.

After proving one of the best bumper performers of his generation, Yorkhill had no difficulty making a winning hurdling debut at Punchestown last December, and he again landed the odds on his next start, when dropped back to two miles in the Tolworth Novices' Hurdle at Sandown in January. Next up was the Neptune Novices' Hurdle at the Cheltenham Festival, when Yorkhill was sent off 3/1 second choice behind the British 'banker' Yanworth. The pair dominated the latter stages, though not in the predicted order—Yorkhill, having tanked along under a patient ride, showed a smart turn of foot to assert early in the straight and had a length and three-quarters to spare come the line (despite idling a shade late on). Yorkhill was back to odds-on for his next outing in the Mersey Novices' at Aintree and completed his Grade 1 hat-trick (and his seventh straight win overall, including an Irish point) by two and a quarter lengths from Le Prezien, though not without scare as his jumping was rather shoddy and he pulled hard too. That wasn't the only time Yorkhill has shown some wayward traits, admittedly, but the positives far outweigh any negatives at this stage and there is potential for better still to come, particularly as he seems versatile with regards

Yorkhill wins the Neptune Novices' Hurdle at Cheltenham

to both ground and trip. Yorkhill is bred to stay at least three miles, but he clearly isn't short of speed and it wouldn't be a surprise to see him emulate his yard's 2014 Neptune winner Faugheen by being campaigned at the minimum trip initially out of the novice stage. Connections have yet to decide whether Yorkhill will be kept over hurdles or tackle fences instead in 2016/17—he's prominent in the betting for both the Arkle and Champion Hurdle at the 2017 Cheltenham Festival—but he's very much one to follow whichever route is chosen for him. ***Willie Mullins***

Conclusion: *Winner at the 2016 Cheltenham and Aintree Festivals and easily forgiven defeat at Punchestown; remains full of potential and can make a big impact out of novice company, whether that be over hurdles or fences; bred to stay 3m but not short of speed*

SECTION

TALKING TO THE TRAINERS

To give some pointers for the new season, we asked a number of leading National Hunt trainers to pick out a star performer, handicapper and dark horse to follow from their respective stables. Read on to find out what names came back...

Nicky Henderson

Wins-Runs in Britain in 2015/16	81/414
Highest-rated horse in training	Sprinter Sacre Timeform Rating c179

Star Performer Altior (h167p) 'We have thought long and hard over the summer as to which route to take and have decided that, although it is tempting to stay over hurdles and see if he is a Champion Hurdle prospect, we are going to take the alternative road and go novice chasing. We did school him in the spring and he has grown considerably during the summer and looks every inch a chaser.'

Handicapper Vyta du Roc (c144+) 'He had a good first season over fences and I am hopeful that he can progress into being a high-class staying handicap chaser.'

Dark Horse Jenkins (b116+) 'He was a pretty smart bumper horse last season, winning very impressively at Newbury and then finishing second in the Land Rover bumper at Punchestown. He will go novice hurdling and has schooled very well.'

Philip Hobbs

Wins-Runs in Britain in 2015/16	113/523
Highest-rated horse in training	Menorah Timeform Rating c166x

Star Performer Westend Story (b116p) 'He won his first two starts in bumpers before finishing fifth in the Champion Bumper at Cheltenham. He looks a good prospect for the season and will start off in a novice hurdle over two and a half miles.'

Handicapper Braavos (h125) 'He only made his hurdling debut last November and won twice once switched to handicaps, at Exeter in January and Perth in April, before finishing a good second to Starchitect at Newton Abbot. He's still improving and capable of winning a decent handicap hurdle before he goes novice chasing.'

Dark Horse Perform (h138p) 'He's a seven-year-old but has run only twice due to minor problems. He won a maiden hurdle at Aintree from two next-time-out winners [including Knockgraffon] when last seen last October and could be a big improver this season.'

Dan Skelton

Wins-Runs in Britain in 2015/16	104/529
Highest-rated horse in training	Al Ferof Timeform Rating c168

Star Performer Three Musketeers (c147) 'Al Ferof is probably our best horse but everyone knows he goes well fresh and he's eleven now, so may not run too many times, whereas Three Musketeers is likely to see more action. He's still only six and we've always trained him as if he's going to improve this season, when the step up to three miles should suit him. He's got to bridge a gap between where he is now and the top level, but we think we've left room for improvement.'

Handicapper Mister Miyagi (h147) 'He finished sixth in the Supreme at the Cheltenham Festival in March but the step up to two and a half miles saw him in a good light when he won there in April. We think the new trip should really help him this time around and we hope he's on a good opening handicap mark of 147.'

Dark Horse Kasakh Noir (h132p) 'He's a horse we can see improving this season as he's a bit older and stronger. He held his form well after coming from France last year, winning twice and finishing sixth in the Fred Winter, and we like him.'

David Pipe

Wins-Runs in Britain in 2015/16	80/571
Highest-rated horse in training	Un Temps Pour Tout Timeform Rating c161

Star Performer Un Temps Pour Tout (c161) 'He was great when winning the Grade 3 Ultima Handicap Chase at the Cheltenham Festival in March. He could start off this year in the Hennessy at Newbury although he may have a prep run before that. It takes a good one to beat him on his day.'

Handicapper La Vaticane (c140) 'La Vaticane hopefully has more to come. She loves the mud and her best form has been over two and a half miles, though a step up to three miles could yet bring further improvement.'

Dark Horse Ramses de Teillee 'He's a four year old by Martaline who has had a couple of starts in Irish point-to-points, winning the second of them in good style. He has summered well and could start off in a bumper before going novice hurdling.'

Harry Fry

Wins-Runs in Britain in 2015/16	54/240
Highest-rated horse in training	**Activial** Timeform Rating h152

Star Performer Unowhatimeanharry (h147p) 'He will be campaigned in staying hurdles, starting off at Wetherby at the end of October. We obviously hope he can develop into a World Hurdle contender.'

Handicapper Thomas Brown (c136) 'He's rated lower over fences than his hurdles mark [Timeform-rated 142] but we think he has the potential to be every bit as good if not better over the larger obstacles. He will start off at Ascot in the Sodexo Gold Cup on 29th October.'

Dark Horse Hell's Kitchen (h132) 'He's a big, imposing five-year-old that we think can go on and be a very decent chaser. He will start off in a beginners chase at the beginning of November.'

Warren Greatrex

Wins-Runs in Britain in 2015/16	53/254
Highest-rated horse in training	**One Track Mind** Timeform Rating h160

Star Performer One Track Mind (h160) 'He won his Grade 1 at Punchestown [Champion Stayers' Hurdle] at the end of last season and will go novice chasing this time around. He could make up into a top-class chaser.'

Handicapper Fly du Charmil (b107 h?) 'He won his bumper at Newbury last November. In hindsight that pretty much finished him for the season, so we think we can forgive his low-key start over hurdles [hasn't been given a BHA mark yet]. He's still a baby and will continue to improve.'

Dark Horse Carnspindle (b84+) 'She finished fourth in her only bumper at Sligo in May when trained by Stuart Crawford. It was against the boys and the form has worked out with the third Golden Poet winning next time. She's done well over the summer and could really improve as the season goes on.'

Kim Bailey

Wins-Runs in Britain in 2015/16	43/275
Highest-rated horse in training	**The Last Samuri** Timeform Rating c158+

Star Performer Charbel (h150) 'He has grown and hopefully improved over the summer. He finished fifth in the Supreme Novices' Hurdle last season and we may take in something like the Elite Hurdle at Wincanton to see where we rank over hurdles before heading over fences. We're very happy with his physical progress.'

Handicapper Younevercall (h134) 'He won two novice hurdles last season, including at Huntingdon, and he was also set to go close when falling at the last there. He must go right-handed and will return in a handicap hurdle at Ascot on the 29th October. We think there is a big prize in him and he goes very well fresh.'

Dark Horse Laval Noir (b107) 'He won a five-runner bumper at Huntingdon by six lengths on his only start. He's schooled very well since and, physically, has improved more than any horse we have.'

Oliver Sherwood

Wins-Runs in Britain in 2015/16	32/207
Highest-rated horse in training	**Many Clouds** Timeform Rating c166

Star Performer Many Clouds (c166) 'He only came back to us in mid-September and we had his soft palate cauterized; we reported after the Grand National that he suffered a breathing problem, while the soft ground over that extreme trip didn't help, either. He's back in routine work and the early signs are good—he's full of the joys of autumn and pulling his lad's arms out on the gallops. We haven't made a firm plan for him yet, though there's a good chance we'll go for that same listed race at Aintree he contested last year. Obviously, all roads will lead to the Grand National again after that.'

Handicapper Legend Lady (h113p) 'She's had a blip or two, hence the reason she only ran twice last season, with nearly three months between runs, but she's a mare we've always liked. If we can keep her on the right path then she can win handicaps, starting on a mark of 114.'

Dark Horse Toberdowney (b87+) 'She's a nice mare who won a Perth bumper in July on her only start for the Crawfords, the same yard from where we got The Organist; if she has a similar level of ability to that mare—and the early signs are positive—then she'll do well this season.'

FIND BETS FASTER AND SMARTER

FILTER

Create a list of horses to bet on today with free **My Timeform Filter**.

Narrow the fields based on criteria you judge to be most important.

Pick the best over course, distance, going, your favourite jockey and more. All at the touch of a button!

At timeform.com and on the App

RISING STARS
Kerry Lee

Base	**Presteigne, Powys**
First Full Licence	**2015**
First Jumps Winner	**Jayo Time** Uttoxeter 09/09/2015
Total Winners	**29** (inc. 2 in Ireland)
Best Horse Trained	**Top Gamble** Timeform Rating c160

Kerry Lee picks up the trophy after the success of Mountainous in the Welsh National

First-season trainer Kerry Lee soon became a familiar face to television viewers thanks to a series of big-race Saturday winners in the early months of 2016. Formerly employed by Channel 4 Racing behind the scenes, she took over the licence at the family's stables on the border between Wales and England on the retirement of her father Richard at the end of the 2014/15 season having assisted in the running of the yard from an early age. With a thirty-horse string, Lee set out with three ambitions in her first season: 'to improve our strike rate to 20%; to send out twenty winners; and to saddle a winner at one of the big festivals in the spring.' It was mission accomplished in all respects, with a total of twenty-three wins in Britain (plus two in Ireland), all bar three of which were gained in chases. Unusually for a stable of modest size, the yard wasn't reliant on a single stable star to keep it in the headlines. A handful of different horses all made significant contributions to a prize-money total which put the stable among the top thirty in the country. Those two Irish wins came courtesy of a graded-race double at the Irish Grand National meeting at Fairyhouse, when Kylemore Lough completed a five-timer in the Grade 1 Ryanair Gold Cup Novices' Chase and the Game Spirit winner Top Gamble won another Grade 2 in the Normans Grove Chase. Back in Britain, the stable completed a notable hat-trick in valuable staying handicaps with Mountainous in the rescheduled Welsh National (repeating his success in the same race two years earlier), Russe Blanc in the Classic Chase at Warwick and the ex-Irish Bishops Road in the Grand National Trial at Haydock. Another who thrived on joining the yard was Jayo Time who was picked up from a claiming hurdle at Worcester in the summer and improved enough over fences to be the trainer's first runner at the Cheltenham Festival.

Trainer's View: "**Kylemore Lough (c156p)** was brilliant for us last season. After improving markedly for his first run he won five times, culminating in a Grade 1 success at Fairyhouse, which made him the winning most performer at Bell House in 2015/16. Bred by his part-owner, Mick McMahon, he's a strapping gelding and has a huge appetite for racing. He has plenty of speed but may start off over two and a half miles and plans are fluid for him. **Mountainous (c139)** is now an eleven-year-old but is still giving every sign he's as good as ever. Everyone knows he loves the mud, and he'll be heading to Chepstow in late-December to defend his Welsh National crown, a race he also won in 2013. He's very tough and could have his prep run at any of Chepstow, Exeter or Sandown. **Russe Blanc (c132)** is the only officially registered white horse in training and has ability to go with his striking looks. He gave us another big winner last season when winning the Classic Chase at Warwick in January, and he thrives on deep ground. He's ideally suited by a stiff, uphill finish and also goes well at both Carlisle and Exeter. A return to Warwick and/or a trip to Ireland look likely for him. **Goodtoknow (c138)** is a horse who took time to mature, flourishing in the latter half of last season when scoring on consecutive starts at Wetherby and Taunton. He has struck up an impressive partnership with Jake Greenall and may be one for Wetherby's Rownland Meyrick Chase at Christmas time. If he continues to improve then perhaps the Irish or Scottish National could turn out to be an end-of-season target. **Grey Gold (c150)** is a real favourite in the yard. He will continue to be ultra-competitive towards the top of the weights in 0-150 handicap chases at the likes of Sandown, Chepstow and Newbury. He looks every bit as good as when winning the Jim Joel Chase at the Hennessy meeting last November and a return for that race looks likely."

Mark Walford

Base	**Sherriff Hutton, North Yorkshire**
First Full Licence	**2014**
First Jumps Winner	**Barleycorn Lady** Newcastle 05/04/2014
Total Winners	**52** (inc. 17 on the Flat)
Best Horse Trained	**Fentara** Timeform Rating c133

Dorset trainer Robert Walford featured in this section of *Horses To Follow* three years ago and now it's the turn of his younger brother Mark who has also made a promising start to his training career since retiring from riding. Having ridden out for neighbour Mick Easterby when still at school, Mark Walford went on to success both in point-to-points and under Rules, riding more than eighty winners as an amateur. Walford began his training career as Pupil Assistant to Mick Channon before returning to Yorkshire for a two-year spell as Assistant Trainer to John Quinn. Swapping roles with his father Tim whom he formerly assisted, Walford took over the licence at Cornborough Manor in 2014 and has since sent out more than fifty winners, most over jumps but also some on the Flat, too. His first winner came in April 2014 and was followed just two days later by an across-the-card double with Cornborough on the Flat at Redcar and Fentara over fences at Kelso—the mare Fentara had also provided Walford with his final winner as a jockey in 2012. Walford had eighteen winners in the calendar year in 2014, a total he repeated in 2015, and has made a fine start to the current jumping campaign with ten winners racked up by the end of August (at a strike-rate of 25%). Cornborough has contributed two of those wins over hurdles, as has new recruit Mountainside, another fairly useful hurdler, while dual Uttoxeter winner Big Sound has struck up a good partnership over fences with stable amateur Emma Todd. Like Kerry Lee, Mark Walford is a young trainer to keep on your side in 2016/17.

Harry Cobden

Attached Stable	**Paul Nicholls**
First Ride	**2015**
First Winner	**El Mondo** Leicester 06/03/2015
Total Winners	**42**
Best Jumps Horse Ridden	**Virak** Timeform Rating c159

We highlighted Sean Bowen as a young jockey to follow in the 2014/15 edition of this book and he went on to win the champion conditional rider's title, and we're sure that another young rider at the Paul Nicholls yard, Harry Cobden, should be followed this season. Cobden initially gained riding experience in the hunting and point fields, gaining plenty of success in the latter discipline in the short time he spent as an amateur, becoming champion novice point-to-point rider at the first attempt. Cobden rode a winner on his first ride under Rules when 33/1-shot El Mondo won a hunter chase at Leicester in March 2015, and he didn't have to wait long for his next winner when Ulck du Lin won a handicap chase at Wincanton on Cobden's third ride. Cobden was attached to the Anthony Honeyball yard at the time—El Mondo was trained by Honeyball's partner Rachael Green and also carried her colours—but Ulck du Lin (who'd actually been ridden to another success earlier in the season by Sean Bowen claiming 7 lb) was trained by Paul Nicholls. More rides for the champion trainer were to follow for Cobden, including on Old Guard who won a conditional jockeys' handicap hurdle at Cheltenham last October under Cobden and then provided the jockey with his biggest win to date in the seventeen-runner Greatwood Handicap Hurdle over the same course and distance the following month. It was the second year in a row that a Paul Nicholls-trained horse had won the race ridden by a 7-lb claimer after Brampour scored under Harry Derham in 2014. Cobden did particularly well on Old Guard in the Greatwood as the horse was keen in the early stages, but Cobden still managed to reserve enough energy for the final charge up the hill, eventually winning by two lengths from Superb Story who would frank the form. Many more winners have followed for the very promising Cobden and, while it sounds rather blasé to say that horses just seem to run for Cobden, he clearly has plenty of natural talent for riding racehorses. What's more, backing all of his rides under Rules so far would have produced a level-stakes profit of over £600 to a £10 level stake. There's no doubt that seventeen-year-old Harry Cobden is a rising star of the weighing room.

Donagh Meyler

Attached Stable	Tony Martin
First Ride	2012
First Winner	**Anibale Fly** Navan 01/03/2015
Total Winners	39
Best Jumps Horse Ridden	**Lord Scoundrel** Timeform Rating c159

Over in Ireland, Donagh Meyler is rapidly making a name for himself in a country that has more than its fair share of promising young jockeys. Like Cobden, Meyler has for a while produced impressive numbers when it comes to the Timeform jockey metrics, so much so that he's rated at least as good as a large proportion of professional riders, even without his allowance factored in. With that in mind, we certainly weren't surprised to see Donagh Meyler ride a significant winner this summer, with the Gigginstown-owned Lord Scoundrel giving the 5-lb claimer the biggest success of his career when landing the Galway Plate. It was the third year in a row the Galway Plate had been won by one of the most promising members of the next generation of jump jockeys, with Shane Shortall winning on Road To Riches in 2014 and Jonathan Burke scoring on Shanahan's Turn in 2015. Meyler wasn't a stranger to landing good-quality handicaps, either, as he'd won such races over hurdles with Mrs Mac Veale at Naas last November and Last Goodbye at Cork in March, and over fences on Colms Dream at Leopardstown in February. Meyler has actually won five times (and also finished second in the valuable Guinness Handicap Chase at Punchestown) on Colms Dream from just eight rides on the horse, and it was particularly impressive the way he was able to help Colms Dream jump fluently at Leopardstown after he'd fallen on his previous two outings (under a different jockey most recently). All four of Meyler's big handicap victories have come for different trainers—including Gordon Elliott in the case of Lord Scoundrel—and none of them for his boss Tony Martin, but it's only a matter of time before that trainer utilizes Meyler to full advantage. Perhaps there are more opportunities for conditional riders in Ireland than there are in Britain—see the aforementioned Jonathan Burke, Danny Mullins and Adrian Heskin all getting big jobs at an early stage of their careers—and that could increase with the retirement of Paul Carberry and the possibility that Ruby Walsh and Barry Geraghty may be more selective of the rides they take in the coming seasons in order to prolong their careers. It would be no surprise to see Meyler take up a retainer with a prominent owner/stable in the coming years given the major impression he's made in his fairly short career so far.

ANTE-POST BETTING

Timeform's Features Writer John Ingles takes a look at the markets for the feature races in the National Hunt calendar and picks out some value bets…

You won't necessarily get paid out of course, but it can feel like a major achievement just for your ante-post bet to actually line up for the race you had backed it for months earlier. The various pitfalls of ante-post involvement were vividly illustrated in a 2015/16 season in which injury ruled out both the reigning Champion Hurdle and Gold Cup winners from defending their titles; when the Champion Hurdle was won by a horse who wasn't even entered in the race to begin with; when a leading Gold Cup contender was switched at the last minute to the Ryanair; when the King George VI and the Queen Mother Champion Chase were both won by horses whose days of winning big races looked over; and when the Grand National was won by a horse who had never won a race over fences before! Somehow, though, all eight of the horses selected here last year made it to their designated races, and one of them, Thistlecrack, gave ante-post backers few anxious moments when winning the World Hurdle, having been advised on these pages at 25/1. Let's hope these selections can prove equally adept at avoiding walking under ladders and treading on stones in the coming months…

King George VI Chase

Last year's King George fought out by **Cue Card** and **Vautour** was one of the races of the season, the pair left clear by the departure two out of Don Cossack who may well have beaten them both had he stood up. Don Cossack's setback means he won't be ready in time to atone for that fall in this year's race, which makes last year's principals the obvious pair to concentrate on again. There was just a head between them in the end, but most lists make Vautour favourite to avenge that defeat. We opposed Vautour last year on the basis that he was unproven at three miles and, to some extent, he still is, not having tackled the trip again since last Boxing Day, though it was the strong pace he set on that occasion, rather than a lack of stamina as such, that counted against him in the end. Cue Card may be the elder of the two, but he was better than ever last term, and, like Vautour, can be excused for ending his campaign on a low note at Punchestown. Unless **Douvan** turns up (he'd presumably do so only in the absence of the same connections' Vautour), last year's first and second set a standard which the other leading chasers are going to struggle to reach, at least at that stage of the season. The 2015 Gold Cup winner **Coneygree** is the only other contender at single-figure odds but has a long absence to overcome after beating his two opponents with ease on his only appearance last season. A front-runner whose interests would be best served by making it a thorough test of stamina, Coneygree's possible presence in the line-up won't make life any easier for Vautour, and Cue Card, at a general 9/2 (5/1 in places), looks the better value of the pair to repeat his 2015 success, hopefully taking in the Charlie Hall and Betfair Chase again along the way.

SELECTION Cue Card (9/2)

Champion Hurdle

The last two winners, **Faugheen** and **Annie Power**, are disputing favouritism in the Champion Hurdle market after Annie Power (who wasn't entered for the race originally) successfully deputised for her injured stable-companion last March. Faugheen's injury was said not to be that serious and Willie Mullins expects his 2015 winner to return "as good as new". Assuming he does, a second Champion Hurdle could easily be his for the taking as he departed the scene looking better than ever when taking his record to eleven out of twelve in the Irish Champion Hurdle in January—his only defeat so far was inflicted by another stablemate, subsequent Champion Hurdle third **Nichols Canyon**, in the Morgiana Hurdle last November. Both owned by Rich and Susannah Ricci, the one apparent certainty regarding Faugheen and Annie Power is that either one or the other, not both, would line up in another Champion Hurdle making neither an attractive ante-post proposition guessing which it will be. Besides the World Hurdle, the Mares' Hurdle is always another option for Annie Power, as it could be again for the same connections' **Vroum Vroum Mag**, the latest winner of that race, who again proved an able deputy for Annie Power in the Punchestown Champion Hurdle. If those aren't enough options already for the Mullins stable, there are last season's leading novices **Min** and **Yorkhill** at slightly longer odds, though a switch to fences probably beckons for both. **Apple's Jade**, on the other hand, is very much in the mix after her Grade 1 wins in the juvenile hurdles at Aintree (in devastating fashion on soft ground) and Punchestown. But on offer at twice her odds (20/1 in most places) is the only horse to have beaten her so far. On good ground at Cheltenham, **Ivanovich Gorbatov** was well on top of Apple's Jade in the Triumph Hurdle and given similar conditions which evidently suit him well, he offers a sound each-way alternative to a Mullins team which will doubtless be strong but whose exact make-up is far from clear at this stage. **Altior** looked a much-needed leading British-trained candidate for the Champion Hurdle when beating Min in the Supreme Novices' but he will reportedly go novice chasing instead.

SELECTION Ivanovich Gorbatov (20/1 each-way)

Queen Mother Champion Chase

A two-horse race if the ante-post market is to be believed, with outstanding novice **Douvan** a best-priced even-money chance against reigning champion **Sprinter Sacre** whom we were guilty of writing off a little too soon in this piece last year. Sprinter Sacre's unlikely comeback to win this race for the second time was one of the stories of last season, but while he proved too good for **Un de Sceaux** at Sandown, as well as at Cheltenham, coping with the latest Willie Mullins-trained Arkle winner Douvan could well be another matter. The chaser with the most potential to rival the sort of ratings Sprinter Sacre himself achieved in his prime,

God's Own leads over the last in Aintree's Melling Chase

Douvan would doubtless be a much shorter price if this was definitely his Cheltenham target and, as things stand, this looks a contest best approached from an each-way angle, taking one of those at longer prices. **God's Own** was fourth to Sprinter Sacre in March but improved on that to win the Melling at Aintree and the Champion Chase at Punchestown, underlining he's very much a spring horse. He appeals at a best price of 20/1, while a riskier each-way proposition at longer odds (33/1) is **Traffic Fluide** who clearly hasn't been easy for Gary Moore to train but has youth on his side. The six-year-old shaped very well on his only start last term when almost depriving stable-companion **Sire de Grugy** of second in the Clarence House Chase won by Un de Sceaux and looks capable of better still given a clean bill of health.

SELECTION God's Own (20/1 each-way)

World Hurdle

Reigning champ in this division, **Thistlecrack**, is predictably favourite to retain his title but he'd be a fair bit shorter than 4/1 if this was his main target. Instead, though, his sights are set on the Gold Cup (see below), so taking that price at best about him in a race that is only a fall-back option in the event of his not taking to fences (and there's always the RSA even if he doesn't make the Gold Cup) makes him a lot less appealing than he was at this time last year. Also predictably, this market is swamped by all the Mullins-trained star hurdlers, even though, surprisingly, the stable wasn't represented at all in last year's World Hurdle, a race Mullins has yet to win. They look to have more than enough firepower to mount a challenge next March, however, and if **Annie Power**, **Faugheen** and **Vroum Vroum Mag** are all fit by then, surely one of that Ricci trio will be assigned to this race. The latter pair have both won over three miles, but the one who appeals most is Annie Power who has a score settle here, meeting her only defeat in completed starts when runner-up to More of That in the 2014 World Hurdle. She didn't fail through lack of stamina that day, simply coming up against a top-class rival, and she evidently had the race as her target again last year until switched to replace Faugheen in the Champion Hurdle. She certainly makes more appeal at 7/1 (8/1 in places) than stablemate **Nichols Canyon** (10/1) whom she beat hollow over two and a half miles at Aintree and who then didn't appear to stay three miles in America in May. Another stable-companion, **Shaneshill**, doesn't have the same star quality, but he has a fine Festival record (runner-up all three starts there) and gets a positive mention, having run some decent races when put back over hurdles in the spring, chasing home Thistlecrack at Aintree and looking the probable winner when falling at the last in the Champion Stayers' Hurdle (won by **One Track Mind**

Annie Power is foot-perfect at the last en-route to victory in the Champion Hurdle

who appears set for chasing this term) at Punchestown. **Jezki** is another former Champion Hurdle winner well up in the betting, though he's been absent through injury since winning the 2015 World Series Hurdle at Punchestown.

SELECTION Annie Power (7/1)

Cheltenham Gold Cup

Even **Thistlecrack**'s biggest fans could be forgiven for wondering what he's doing at the head of the Gold Cup betting without having jumped a fence in public. Of course, there's a recent precedent for a novice winning the Gold Cup—2015 winner **Coneygree** isn't far down the lists to win it again—but Thistlecrack, for all his top-class form in staying hurdles and his chaser's build, will have to prove at least as good over fences in just a handful of starts at most—beating two or three rivals in a novice chase at Exeter or Chepstow to begin with won't mean much in the context of a Gold Cup picture which doesn't exactly represent easy pickings at present. Coneygree won't be the only former winner attempting a return from injury, though—**Don Cossack** would surely be favourite to retain his crown were it not for his setback since last March—while Thistlecrack's stable-companion **Cue**

Card (who fell when bang there three out last season) makes more appeal at this stage at 10/1 than the favourite at 7/1. Willie Mullins has still to win the Gold Cup but he's unlikely to be short of options in 2017. **Vautour** is challenging Thistlecrack for favouritism but those who had their fingers burned by his late and unexpected switch to the Ryanair instead are unlikely to be rushing in again, particularly with the same owner's potential superstar **Douvan** now on the scene as well in addition to **Djakadam** who's been runner-up for the Riccis in the last two years. **Valseur Lido** and last season's third **Don Poli** are two more Mullins possibles, but the Gigginstown-owned pair would only be playing second fiddle to Don Cossack if their owner's Gold Cup winner is back in good order by next March. Douvan apart, last season's novice chasers look up against it if they're to challenge the established leading staying chasers, but one who may have the potential to do so is yet another from the Mullins stable **Killultagh Vic**. The fact he was injured after making it two from two over fences last winter means he's not without risks (he was favourite for the JLT at the Festival at the time, which was won instead by stable-companion **Black Hercules**), but he's looked a natural over fences and did really well to win a Grade 2 novice contest at Leopardstown after almost slithering to a standstill on landing over the last. A former Festival winner over hurdles (the 2015 Martin Pipe), Killultagh Vic will be suited by a return to three miles, and don't forget he was the last horse to beat Thistlecrack over hurdles when successful at Punchestown in April 2015.

SELECTION Killultagh Vic (25/1 each-way)

Grand National

Last season's Grand National winner, Rule The World, has been retired but his trainer Mouse Morris and owner Gigginstown House Stud have another possible candidate for the 2017 race in the form of **Rogue Angel**, winner of the Irish Grand National last March, a race in which Rule The World had himself been runner-up twelve months before going one better at Aintree. The other Gigginstown chaser prominent in the betting is **Don Poli** who certainly shapes as though long distances will suit him and boasts top-class form (runner-up to Cue Card in the Bowl at the latest National meeting after finishing third in the Gold Cup), though he will be weighted accordingly in what could be his first handicap over fences. Last season's top weight, **Many Clouds**, will presumably make another bid to become the first since Red Rum to win the race again (he reportedly had a breathing problem when trailing home last behind Rule The World after going well until a blunder five out), while the other joint-favourite last April, **The Last Samuri**, would attempt to emulate Red Rum by being the first Grand National runner-up to go one better twelve months later if taking his chance again. The Last Samuri won't have the same chance at the weights as he did last season, but it's no surprise he's favourite in many lists given that he took so well to the demands of the race, jumping superbly and seeing the trip out well. Also vying for favouritism is **The Young Master** who looks a likely Aintree type after ending last term with victory in the bet365 Gold Cup at Sandown under amateur Sam Waley-Cohen, who has such a good record over the National fences.

Our selections, though, are headed by **Minella Rocco** who became owner J. P. McManus' latest winner of the National Hunt Chase at Cheltenham in which he was chased home by subsequent Mildmay Novices' winner **Native River**. Minella Rocco will still be only seven next year—and the last horse aged under eight to win the race was Bogskar in 1940—but stamina is clearly his strong suit, and he seems sure to improve further given how little racing he has had. McManus has other possibles, including Punchestown Gold Cup winner **Carlingford Lough**, dual Festival winner **Cause of Causes** (eighth in the 2015 National but not high enough in the weights to get in last time), last season's National fourth **Gilgamboa** and one of our selections last year, **Gallant Oscar**, who was shaping well when unseating (after a heroic effort from Mark Walsh to try to keep the partnership intact—have another watch) on the second circuit and could well be of interest again. Our second selection, though, is **Vicente** who was fifth to Minella Rocco at Cheltenham before going on to win the Scottish National. By Dom Alco, the sire of Paul Nicholls' 2012 Grand National winner Neptune Collonges, Vicente can also boast good form from earlier in the season when he won a novice at Cheltenham conceding weight to future Festival winners Un Temps Pour Tout and Blaklion. Another we like the look of at a massive 66/1 each-way is **Henri Parry Morgan** who jumped well before unseating late on when favourite for the bet365 Gold Cup. His trainer Peter Bowen has an excellent record at Aintree (went close with McKelvey in the National in 2007) and Henri Parry Morgan ran well there himself when second in the Mildmay.

SELECTION Minella Rocco and Vicente (both 33/1), Henri Parry Morgan (66/1 each way)

SECTION

TIMEFORM'S VIEW

Chosen from the Timeform Formbook, here is Timeform's detailed analysis—compiled by our team of race reporters and supplemented by observations from Timeform's handicappers—of a selection of key races from the Cheltenham, Aintree and Punchestown festivals last spring.

CHELTENHAM Tuesday March 15
GOOD

Sky Bet Supreme Novices' Hurdle (Grade 1) (1) 2m 87y

Pos	Btn	Horse	Age	Wgt	Eq	Trainer	Jockey	SP
1		ALTIOR (IRE)	6	11-7		Nicky Henderson	Nico de Boinville	4/1
2	7	MIN (FR)	5	11-7		W. P. Mullins, Ireland	R. Walsh	15/8f
3	1½	BUVEUR D'AIR (FR)	5	11-7		Nicky Henderson	Noel Fehily	10/1
4	4	TOMBSTONE (IRE)	6	11-7		Gordon Elliott, Ireland	B. J. Cooper	12/1
5	hd	CHARBEL (IRE)	5	11-7	(t)	Kim Bailey	David Bass	16/1
6	1¼	MISTER MIYAGI (IRE)	7	11-7		Dan Skelton	Ian Popham	33/1
7	sh	SUPASUNDAE	6	11-7		Henry de Bromhead, Ireland	J. J. Burke	12/1
8	1	PETIT MOUCHOIR (FR)	5	11-7	(h)	W. P. Mullins, Ireland	David Mullins	20/1
9	9	NORTH HILL HARVEY	5	11-7		Dan Skelton	Harry Skelton	25/1
10	3	WILLIAM H BONNEY	5	11-7		Alan King	Wayne Hutchinson	50/1
11	1½	HOLLY BUSH HENRY (IRE)	5	11-7	(t)	Graeme McPherson	Kielan Woods	40/1
12	¾	PENGLAI PAVILION (USA)	6	11-7		John Ferguson	Aidan Coleman	33/1
13	2¼	BELLSHILL (IRE)	6	11-7		W. P. Mullins, Ireland	P. Townend	11/1
14	hd	SILVER CONCORDE	8	11-7		D. K. Weld, Ireland	Davy Russell	16/1

14 ran Race Time 3m 46.50 Closing Sectional (3.90f): 53.0s (101.6%) Winning Owner: Mrs Patricia Pugh

An outstanding novice performance ended the Willie Mullins' domination of the Supreme, Altior's display well up to the recent standard for the race, which given that Vautour and Douvan were the last 2 winners is some standard to match, the winning margin a length further than Vautour managed and the widest since Back In Front beat Kicking King in 2003; the pace was a bit slower than for the Champion Hurdle later on the card and the race developed only from 3 out, testing speed more than stamina, the form, with the possible exception of Mister Miyagi, looking very solid. **Altior** looked out of the top drawer tried at the highest level, making it 5 from 5 over hurdles with the minimum of fuss, his speed just too much in the closing stages for the favourite; in touch, travelled well, went handy 2 out, led under pressure early in straight, quickened clear approaching last, kept on well run-in, impressive; he's an obvious candidate, if all goes well, to make a leading contender in top 2m hurdle races next winter. **Min** had been all the rage for this for much of the winter and, though he came up short on the day, still ran well, likely beaten only by a top-notch 2-miler; prominent, travelled well, mistake third, led briefly after 2 out, not quicken before last, kept on run-in; he has the physique of a chaser and it would be no surprise to see him back here in 2017 as a leading candidate for the Arkle. **Buveur d'Air** matched previous form, and might have finished second had his effort begun sooner, not so well placed as the runner-up when the race began to develop; held up, smooth headway before 2 out, ridden after, kept on well straight, nearest at the finish; he's a prospective smart novice chaser for next season, though could well get another chance at this level over hurdles at Aintree or Punchestown first. **Tombstone** on less testing ground than previously, ran well, needing no excuses, though he was keener than ideal, without the hood this time; prominent, not settle fully, effort before 2 out, kept on straight; he ought to make at least as good a chaser next winter. **Charbel** ran creditably in first-time tongue strap, confirming himself a smart novice and a likely sort, on physique if not on pedigree, for making at least as good a novice chaser next season; led, pushed along approaching 2 out, headed soon after, one paced straight, not fluent last. **Mister Miyagi** after 4 months off, seemed to excel himself up significantly in grade, no obvious reason to think he was flattered, one who clearly benefited from ground less soft than anticipated; held up, mistake first, ridden after 3 out, stayed on straight, nearest at the finish. **Supasundae** after 11 weeks off, proved at least as good as previously despite a sloppy round of jumping, remaining open to improvement with more fluency; prominent, made mistakes, ridden 2 out, one paced. **Petit Mouchoir** proved at least as good as previously, coping with less testing conditions, just not up to this grade; chased leaders, ridden before 2 out, one paced home turn. **North Hill Harvey** had his work cut out in this company, on less testing ground than previously, but he promised more than he finally delivered and may yet do better, this just his fourth start over hurdles; held up, travelled well, headway before 3 out, mistake next, ridden after, found little. **William H Bonney** ran respectably, facing a stiff task in this grade, on much less testing ground than previously; mid-division, labouring 3 out. **Holly Bush Henry** after 8 weeks off, had been most progressive but just wasn't up to this much sterner task; held up, labouring 3 out. **Penglai Pavilion** was well held after 4 months off, finding this too competitive; held up, ridden before 3 out, made no impression. **Bellshill** ran poorly back down in trip, running in the wrong race to accommodate his owner's Yorkhill in the Baring Bingham; waited with, not fluent fourth, weakened after fifth. **Silver Concorde** ran no sort of race after 11 weeks off, presumably not right, conditions not likely to have been a problem given his win in the Champion Bumper; held up, labouring badly fifth.

Racing Post Arkle Challenge Trophy Chase (Grade 1) (1) 1m 7f 199y

Pos	Btn	Horse	Age	Wgt	Eq	Trainer	Jockey	SP
1		DOUVAN (FR)	6	11-4		W. P. Mullins, Ireland	R. Walsh	1/4f
2	7	SIZING JOHN	6	11-4		Henry de Bromhead, Ireland	J. J. Burke	9/1
3	3¾	FOX NORTON (FR)	6	11-4	(h)	Neil Mulholland	Richard Johnson	33/1
4	2¼	THE GAME CHANGER (IRE)	7	11-4	(t)	Gordon Elliott, Ireland	B. J. Cooper	14/1
5	1	ASO (FR)	6	11-4	(s)	Venetia Williams	Aidan Coleman	66/1
F		BALTIMORE ROCK (IRE)	7	11-4	(s+t)	Neil Mulholland	Noel Fehily	40/1
ur		VANITEUX (FR)	7	11-4		Nicky Henderson	Nico de Boinville	8/1

7 ran Race Time 3m 48.70 Closing Sectional (3.65f): 50.8s (103.3%) Winning Owner: Mrs S. Ricci

Douvan had dominated the 2m novice chase scene in Ireland this season and set a very high standard, way in advance of his British counterparts, and he duly proved far too good, making most of the running and winning with plenty in hand; after taking it up soon after the second fence Ruby Walsh was able to dictate an ordinary tempo and the field were still well bunched jumping 3 out, hence why they didn't finish as strung out as they perhaps should have given the respective abilities on show, limiting the view that's taken of the bare form, but Douvan is rated as more superior than the winning margin, that view backed up by his outstanding closing sectional. **Douvan** is up there with the most talented novice chasers of recent times, certainly the standout in the division this season, and, although he didn't need to improve to land this third consecutive Grade 1, yet again he barely came out of second gear and was value for plenty more than the winning margin; tanked along, jumped superbly, led after second and made rest, quickened between 3 out and 2 out, effortlessly drew away, in command last, won easily; the full extent of his ability hasn't been revealed yet but there's no question that Douvan has the potential to put himself in the truly elite bracket, ratings in excess of the mid-170s a distinct possibility, and it'll be hugely exciting to see him contest the top open races next season. **Sizing John** wasn't at his best in the mud 12 weeks ago but these conditions were more his bag and he wasted no time getting back to form, simply not in the same league as Douvan (placed behind him 5 times now) but a smart, likeable type in his own right; led until after second, remained prominent, ridden between 3 out and 2 out, left second 2 out, kept on, no match for winner; it's worth trying him at around 2½m. **Fox Norton** excelled himself in face of his stiffest task to date, producing a career best, suited by the relative emphasis on speed given how the race was run, especially on this stiff course; mid-division, avoided mistakes, pushed along soon after 3 out, kept on without truly threatening either of the first 2; he's probably one for the major 2m handicap chases next season as opposed to the big graded races. **The Game Changer** had been freshened up after a busy first half of the season, arriving here after 5 months off, and shaped better than distance beaten suggests, looking set to finish closer until hampered by Vaniteux's blunder/unseat 2 out; held up, travelled smoothly, pecked second, headway 3 out, keeping on when baulked 2 out, no extra; he's smart and perhaps a flat track like Aintree will see him to very best effect. **Aso** in first-time cheekpieces, wasn't up to the task but ran as well as he was entitled to, though it's likely that he'd have been beaten further if they'd gone a stronger pace; in rear, jumped none too fluently, hit 3 out, struggling soon after, plugged on. **Baltimore Rock** who was fitted with cheekpieces, found this too competitive and, after briefly moving closer 4 out, he'd already been put in his place when crashing out at the second last, that not his first error (hit sixth) either; he may yet do better as a chaser but high-end handicaps are more for him. **Vaniteux** was in the process of running well when departing, likely to have run right up to his best, but he has shown a tendency to hit the odd fence in this novice season over fences (has a fairly low jumping technique) and that side of things needs to improve if he's to win the races he might in this sphere; prominent, went with enthusiasm, challenged after 3 out, blundered and unseated rider next when looking sure to be placed.

Stan James Champion Hurdle Challenge Trophy (Grade 1) (1) 2m 87y

Pos	Btn	Horse	Age	Wgt	Eq	Trainer	Jockey	SP
1		ANNIE POWER (IRE)	8	11-3		W. P. Mullins, Ireland	R. Walsh	5/2f
2	4½	MY TENT OR YOURS (IRE)	9	11-10	(h)	Nicky Henderson	Barry Geraghty	10/1
3	hd	NICHOLS CANYON	6	11-10		W. P. Mullins, Ireland	P. Townend	15/2
4	4	THE NEW ONE (IRE)	8	11-10		Nigel Twiston-Davies	Sam Twiston-Davies	7/2
5	1	TOP NOTCH (FR)	5	11-10		Nicky Henderson	Daryl Jacob	14/1
6	9	IDENTITY THIEF (IRE)	6	11-10		Henry de Bromhead, Ireland	B. J. Cooper	8/1
7	1¼	LIL ROCKERFELLER (USA)	5	11-10	(s)	Neil King	Trevor Whelan	20/1
8	2¾	SIGN OF A VICTORY (IRE)	7	11-10		Nicky Henderson	Andrew Tinkler	66/1
9	nk	CAMPING GROUND (FR)	6	11-10	(t)	Robert Walford	Leighton Aspell	16/1
10	28	HARGAM (FR)	5	11-10		Nicky Henderson	Mark Walsh	16/1
pu		SEMPRE MEDICI (FR)	6	11-10	(t)	W. P. Mullins, Ireland	David Mullins	16/1
pu		PEACE AND CO (FR)	5	11-10		Nicky Henderson	Nico de Boinville	16/1

12 ran Race Time 3m 45.00 Closing Sectional (3.90f): 53.2s (100.6%) Winning Owner: Mrs S. Ricci

The absence through injury of the outstanding 2m hurdler Faugheen, as well as last season's runner-up Arctic Fire, meant this was a substandard renewal of the top 2m hurdle of the season, Annie Power proving an able substitute after being supplemented, not having to improve on her very best form on a rare foray outside races for her own sex; the placed horses ran with credit, with no excuses really, but most of the rest found a well-run race at this level on rather quicker ground than anticipated all too much for them. **Annie Power** who'd been supplemented after Faugheen's injury, didn't need to improve to become the first mare to win this race since Flakey Dove, her performance here and in the 2014 World Hurdle making it rather a shame that she's not been tried more often outside mares events; led first, made rest, jumped/travelled well, drew clear after 2 out, kept on well run-in, won readily; she will presumably stand in for Faugheen at Punchestown as well, and will take all the beating given the likely opposition. **My Tent Or Yours** not seen for nearly 2 years, showed all his old ability remains, a fine training performance to have him at his best after such a long absence, placed at this meeting for the third time; prominent, not settle fully, ridden after 2 out, not quicken approaching last, kept on run-in; presumably a rematch with the winner at Punchestown will be next, if he continues to stand training. **Nichols Canyon** bounced back to form, indeed running his best race yet, likely to have finished second had he not fluffed the last; prominent, mistake third, not quicken 2 out, keeping on when mistake last; he's a high-class hurdler, who will win more races below the very highest level, but is always likely to come up short in a Champion Hurdle, the Aintree Hurdle back up in trip presumably an option next. **The New One** ran creditably, as previously in this race lacking speed at a crucial stage; led until first, remained prominent, plugged on after 2 out; it's surprising he's not run beyond 2m since the 2014 Aintree Hurdle, his close second and a narrow win in 2 tries at that race suggesting strongly that is where he should go next, the World Hurdle the obvious option in a year's time. **Top Notch** ran creditably, with no excuses, this as good as he is as a hurdler, a switch to fences next season the obvious move with him; in touch, effort when mistake 2 out, one paced. **Identity Thief** was below form after 11 weeks off, perhaps just not up to the task, though he had raced on going softer than good previously; chased leaders, not fluent fourth, ridden when not fluent 3 out, left behind home turn. **Lil Rockerfeller** wasn't disgraced, having been supplemented, given 2m in this company on good ground wasn't an ideal test; mid-division, soon off bridle, never on terms. **Sign of A Victory** wasn't disgraced after 12 weeks off, flying too high in this grade and rather flattering to deceive once more; held up, not settle fully, smooth headway 3 out, ridden next, no extra; he'd be better off in something like the Swinton on similar ground. **Camping Ground** back down in trip, was run off his feet, probably better on softer ground anyway; untidy first, badly outpaced long way out, always behind. **Hargam** was well held after 12 weeks off, possibly better on easier ground; waited with, labouring badly third. **Sempre Medici** was well held in first-time tongue strap, flying too high in this grade; held up, labouring fifth, tailed off when pulled up last. **Peace And Co** has had a season of abject disappointment after his Triumph success at this meeting a year ago, hard to know where connections go with him now; raced off the pace, pushed along fifth, carried head awkwardly 3 out, pulled up last.

CHELTENHAM Wednesday March 16
GOOD

Neptune Investment Management Novices' Hurdle (Baring Bingham) (Grade 1) (1) 2m 5f 26y

Pos	Btn	Horse	Age	Wgt	Eq	Trainer	Jockey	SP
1		YORKHILL (IRE)	6	11-7		W. P. Mullins, Ireland	R. Walsh	3/1
2	1¾	YANWORTH	6	11-7		Alan King	Barry Geraghty	11/10f
3	7	ITS'AFREEBEE (IRE)	6	11-7		Dan Skelton	Ian Popham	33/1
4	4	BELLO CONTI (FR)	5	11-7		W. P. Mullins, Ireland	David Mullins	20/1
5	sh	WELSH SHADOW (IRE)	6	11-7		Dan Skelton	Harry Skelton	28/1
6	½	VIGIL (IRE)	7	11-7		D. K. Weld, Ireland	Davy Russell	16/1
7	7	A TOI PHIL (FR)	6	11-7		W. P. Mullins, Ireland	B. J. Cooper	8/1
8	3	O O SEVEN (IRE)	6	11-7		Nicky Henderson	Andrew Tinkler	20/1
9	30	GHOST RIVER	6	11-7		Peter Bowen	Sean Bowen	100/1
pu		THOMAS HOBSON	6	11-7		W. P. Mullins, Ireland	P. Townend	14/1
pu		YALA ENKI (FR)	6	11-7		Venetia Williams	Aidan Coleman	25/1

11 ran Race Time 5m 00.50 Closing Sectional (3.9f): 54.1s (102.6%) Winning Owner: Andrea & Graham Wylie

A race won by a host of top-class horses over the years, The New One and Faugheen both recent winners, and this appeals as a strong renewal, bringing together 2 of the most exciting novice hurdlers around in Yorkhill and Yanworth, and it was that pair that pulled clear despite a pace that hadn't been especially strong, the 2 going further away at the finish and value for beating the rest by even further. **Yorkhill** had looked a fine prospect on each previous start under Rules and maintained his unbeaten record in a deeper Grade 1 than the Tolworth he'd won with something to spare 11 weeks ago, again value for extra, not the sort to do a lot in front, and it was so impressive how he carted himself there soon after the home turn; raced along inside, held up, tanked along, headway when untidy 3 out, led on bridle between last 2, idled run-in (edged right), ridden out; there are so many options for him going forward, no doubt that he has the speed to drop back to 2m, be it for a Champion Hurdle or novice-chase campaign, either way a top-class performer in the making, and nearer to hand there's surely another Grade 1 novice to be won with him. **Yanworth** met with defeat for the first time over hurdles but still ran a belter behind another very exciting novice in Yorkhill, without things going all that smoothly for him, wide throughout while Yorkhill hugged the inner; raced wide, held up, bumped after 4 out, headway when not fluent next, driven before last, ran on, pulled clear of remainder; he remains a top-notch prospect. **Its'afreebee** was in a much tougher race and improved again to be competitive, no shame in being left behind by a pair as promising as Yorkhill and Yanworth, staying the longer trip, probably in his favour on drying ground in fact; pressed leader (briefly short of room and almost forced off track back straight), went on after 3 out, headed between last 2, kept on without being a match for principals; he's very likeable and has the physique/manner of one that'll do well novice chasing next season. **Bello Conti** was light on experience, just once-raced in Ireland, that 12 weeks ago, and he coped with the step up in grade and 3f longer trip, showing improved form to hit the frame in a hot race; held up, pushed along after 3 out, chased leaders next, outpaced before last, kept on; he's still totally unexposed. **Welsh Shadow** unsurprisingly found the company a bit too hot but ran well, showing slight improvement on the form of his Dovecote third, with the 4f longer trip seeming in his favour; held up, blundered fourth, in touch 3 out, not quicken after 2 out; he's one to keep in mind for some of the valuable handicaps at this sort of trip next season (may do better still), as he leaves the impression that a strongly-run race may suit ideally. **Vigil** wasn't up to the task but produced his best effort to date despite still looking rough around the edges as a hurdler; in rear, novicey mistakes, headway under pressure before 2 out, plugged on, never a threat; there's room for improvement in his jumping and if that clicks he'll do even better, a really smart bumper performer of course. **A Toi Phil** is better than this, promising plenty with his 2 wins in Ireland but possibly unsuited by these less testing conditions, perhaps just not ready for a race as competitive as this, either; prominent, bumped after sixth, lost place when mistake 3 out, soon done with. **O O Seven** was below form at this meeting for the second year in succession, possibly not ideally suited to the track; tracked pace, not settle fully, bumped after sixth, challenged 3 out, folded between last 2; he looks a chaser in the making. **Ghost River** was flying too high in this grade; mid-division, went handy before 3 out, struggling next. **Thomas Hobson** clearly wasn't 100% on the day, also possibly unsuited by conditions; made running, made mistakes, took strong hold, headed after 3 out, stopped quickly. **Yala Enki** is best not judged on this run; in touch, shuffled back after second, stumbled fourth, pulled up quickly, something not right.

RSA Chase (Grade 1) (1) 3m 80y

Pos	Btn	Horse	Age	Wgt	Eq	Trainer	Jockey	SP
1		BLAKLION	7	11-4		Nigel Twiston-Davies	Ryan Hatch	8/1
2	½	SHANESHILL (IRE)	7	11-4		W. P. Mullins, Ireland	P. Townend	16/1
3	8	MORE OF THAT (IRE)	8	11-4		Jonjo O'Neill	Barry Geraghty	6/4f
4	¾	NO MORE HEROES (IRE)	7	11-4		Gordon Elliott, Ireland	B. J. Cooper	5/2
5	1¼	VYTA DU ROC (FR)	7	11-4		Nicky Henderson	Daryl Jacob	12/1
6	10	ROI DES FRANCS (FR)	7	11-4		W. P. Mullins, Ireland	R. Walsh	10/1
7	12	SEEYOUATMIDNIGHT	8	11-4		Sandy Thomson	Brian Hughes	9/1
8	2	LE MERCURY (FR)	6	11-4	(s+t)	Paul Nicholls	Sam Twiston-Davies	33/1

8 ran Race Time 6m 05.90 Closing Sectional (3.65f): 54.6s (100.4%) Winning Owner: S Such & CG Paletta

The season's leading staying novice chase and, although there were only 8 runners, it looked a potentially strong renewal with dual Irish Grade-1 winner No More Heroes and former World Hurdle title-holder More of That dominating the market and pre-race ratings ahead of others that had won what are traditionally key trials for this race; as it turned out, though, the standard-setting pair both had problems on the day—sadly, No More Heroes succumbed to his injuries—that meant they didn't perform to their best and, although Blaklion and Shaneshill can be credited with improvement, the form is of a standard a little lower than an average RSA. **Blaklion** might not have the class and potential of some RSA winners before him but certainly has a likeable way of going about things, a sound jumper with a cracking attitude, and he found a bit more improvement to win this premier staying novice prize 6 weeks after ploughing through the mud in the Towto, as versatile as he is reliable; mid-division, crept closer eleventh, shaken up after 3 out, found plenty to lead run-in, driven out; a lot of further progress will be required if he's to mix it in the top open staying events next season, especially with such an array of talent around in that division. **Shaneshill** was up markedly in trip, campaigned around 2m over fences up to now, and, unlike when he'd tried this far over hurdles last season, it seemed to suit him, doing well under the circumstances, coming from a long way back after a mixed round of jumping; in rear, not always fluent but travelled strongly, hit 3 out, rapid headway soon after, challenged 2 out, jumped on last, headed run-in, kept on and clear of the the rest; he's been very good since day one, runner-up in a Champion Bumper and Supreme Novice at the last 2 Festivals, and he remains open to improvement in this sphere, his jumping likely to get better as he gains more experience. **More of That** has had his share of physical problems since winning the World Hurdle 2 years ago and it could be that they're going to hold him back, coming here after 3 months off (which is unlikely to have been the initial plan) and clearly not at his best, reported afterwards to have bled from both nostrils; held up, not always fluent, ridden 3 out, every chance next, one paced. **No More Heroes** could hardly have made a better impression in 3 novice chases in Ireland, and was in with every chance for most of the latter stages, but he met with a sad end, sustaining a tendon injury which meant he subsequently had to be put down. **Vyta du Roc** beat the National Hunt Chase winner, Minella Rocco, at Ascot last month but failed to progress any further from that, still running creditably in this deeper contest; held up, in touch fourteenth, outpaced between 3 out and 2 out, plugged on; he'll be worth a try at further than 3m at some stage. **Roi des Francs** might not have achieved as it much as it seemed with his 2 heavy-ground wins in Ireland, neither of them particularly strong form, and he was well held in this much hotter race on less testing ground; prominent, took strong hold, upsides 3 out, weakening when blundered last, no extra. **Seeyouatmidnight** proved to be a disappointment but is better than this, as his defeat of Blaklion earlier in the season shows, acknowledging that was over a shorter trip and in receipt of weight; led, rare sloppy round of jumping, headed when hit 3 out, soon done with. **Le Mercurey** followed a good run with a below-par one, his profile patchy; chased leaders, lost place soon after 4 out, tailed off; there are signs of temperament and he's worth a try in headgear.

Betway Queen Mother Champion Chase (Grade 1) (1) 1m 7f 199y

Pos	Btn	Horse	Age	Wgt	Eq	Trainer	Jockey	SP
1		SPRINTER SACRE (FR)	10	11-10		Nicky Henderson	Nico de Boinville	5/1
2	3½	UN DE SCEAUX (FR)	8	11-10		W. P. Mullins, Ireland	R. Walsh	4/6f
3	ns	SPECIAL TIARA	9	11-10		Henry de Bromhead, Ireland	Noel Fehily	16/1
4	5	GOD'S OWN (IRE)	8	11-10		Tom George	Paddy Brennan	20/1
5	5	SOMERSBY (IRE)	12	11-10	(s)	Mick Channon	Brian Hughes	50/1
6	9	JUST CAMERON	9	11-10	(t)	Micky Hammond	Joe Colliver	66/1
7	4	DODGING BULLETS	8	11-10	(t)	Paul Nicholls	Sam Twiston-Davies	10/1
8	40	SIRE DE GRUGY (FR)	10	11-10		Gary Moore	Jamie Moore	16/1
pu		FELIX YONGER (IRE)	10	11-10		W. P. Mullins, Ireland	P. Townend	11/1
pu		SIZING GRANITE (IRE)	8	11-10		Colm A. Murphy, Ireland	J. J. Burke	33/1

10 ran Race Time 3m 49.60 Closing Sectional (3.65f): 55.3s (95.3%) Winning Owner: Mrs Caroline Mould

Sprinter Sacre given 11 weeks off since Kempton, made it 3 wins from as many starts this season in landing a second Champion Chase, showing form about 2 stone shy of what he achieved when putting up the greatest chase performance of the modern era in the first one, no longer capable of that sort of outstanding effort but still a top-class chaser, more than a match for the best around at the moment, and it's to the immense credit of his trainer that he's doing this at all mindful of how much has gone wrong for him in the meantime; comfortable with the strong pace, he raced in third for much of the way, jumped well in the main (bit untidy when closing 3 out but produced some spectacular leaps otherwise), took over from the 2 pace-setters approaching 2 out and was well in control when making a slight mistake at the last, nearly 8 lengths up on the run-in, tiring a little up the hill and driven out to make sure; one or more of Aintree, Sandown and Punchestown are options for him this spring, though he may not be the sort to stand too much racing these days, and there's arguably more to be lost than gained in asking him to race again this season. **Un de Sceaux** all the rage in the betting 8 weeks on from another Grade 1 win at Ascot, met with defeat for the first time when completing over fences, coming up short faced with his most meaningful opposition so far in the shape of an on-song Sprinter Sacre, and while it's fair to say this race didn't go all his way, unable to lead with Special Tiara in the field and probably doing a bit much in pursuit of that rival in a strongly-run race, it's a bit of a stretch to suggest that the result would've been a whole lot different had things panned out another way; soon chasing the leader in second, he made small mistakes at the first and fourth, took over going powerfully after 4 out but had no answer once the winner breezed by on the home turn, all out to maintain second on the run-in; it's possible he wasn't quite at his best on the day for some reason, and even if not he's bound to win more good races over fences, especially when able to dominate, though this defeat means there's more of a limit in place with him now, and this division is only going to get tougher next year with his stable-companion Douvan about to come onto the scene. **Special Tiara** ran a cracker after 3 months off, finishing third in this race for the second year running, that despite again doing plenty in front, and there'll be races at this level another time when his trademark trailblazing tactics will be that much easier to pull off, starting in the Celebration Chase at Sandown he won last year on the back of another third in this; made running, pecked third, headed after 4 out, effort before 2 out, kept on. **God's Own** without a tongue strap this time, ran creditably, ridden to pick up the pieces but even then not good enough; held up, headway under pressure 3 out, blundered next, one paced. **Somersby** after 11 weeks off, ran as well as he was entitled to, just not up to this standard any longer; mid-division, shaken up 3 out, blundered 2 out, one paced. **Just Cameron** wasn't disgraced but would've been better off in the Grand Annual; mid-division, not fluent third, behind from 5 out. **Dodging Bullets** won this race last year but has had a far-from-ideal preparation this time around and never looked like repeating the dose, therefore left with a little to prove for now; mid-division, not fluent seventh, hit 5 out, behind from 3 out. **Sire de Grugy** had form this season good enough to get involved (has beaten Special Tiara and finished second to both Sprinter Sacre and Un de Sceaux) but just ran flat-out poorly back from 8 weeks off, something maybe not right for him to perform as he did, always right out the back. **Felix Yonger** found this tougher than the small-field, heavy-ground races he's been winning in Ireland and was done for a long way out after a bad mistake at the second left him with a mountain to climb. **Sizing Granite** had conditions more in his favour on his first outing since leaving Henry De Bromhead after 11 weeks off but made a race-ruining mistake at the first and was tailed off a long way out.

Weatherbys Champion Bumper (Standard Open National Hunt Flat) (Grade 1) (1) 2m 87y

Pos	Btn	Horse	Age	Wgt	Eq	Trainer	Jockey	SP
1		BALLYANDY	5	11-5		Nigel Twiston-Davies	Sam Twiston-Davies	5/1
2	ns	BATTLEFORD	5	11-5		W. P. Mullins, Ireland	M. P. Fogarty	25/1
3	2	BACARDYS (FR)	5	11-5		W. P. Mullins, Ireland	R. Walsh	16/1
4	1	CASTELLO SFORZA (IRE)	5	11-5		W. P. Mullins, Ireland	Barry Geraghty	11/1

5	nk	WESTEND STORY (IRE)	5	11-5		Philip Hobbs	Richard Johnson	20/1
6	1¼	HIGH BRIDGE	5	11-5		John Ferguson	Aidan Coleman	12/1
7	½	AUGUSTA KATE	5	10-12		W. P. Mullins, Ireland	P. Townend	7/2f
8	ns	VERY MUCH SO (IRE)	6	11-5		W. P. Mullins, Ireland	David Mullins	33/1
9	½	FIRST FIGARO (GER)	6	11-5		D. K. Weld, Ireland	Davy Russell	16/1
9	0	RATHER BE (IRE)	5	11-5		Nicky Henderson	Andrew Tinkler	50/1
11	nk	COEUR BLIMEY (IRE)	5	11-5		Susan Gardner	Lucy Gardner	16/1
12	1	AVENIR D'UNE VIE (FR)	6	11-5		W. P. Mullins, Ireland	Mr P. W. Mullins	10/1
13	½	PRIDE OF LECALE	5	11-5	(t)	Fergal O'Brien	Paddy Brennan	50/1
14	5	CRIQ ROCK (FR)	5	11-5		Alan King	Wayne Hutchinson	33/1
15	2½	TURCAGUA (FR)	6	11-5		W. P. Mullins, Ireland	Ms K. Walsh	33/1
16	1½	ONTHEWESTERNFRONT (IRE)	6	11-5		Jonjo O'Neill	Miss N. Carberry	40/1
17	½	COMPADRE (IRE)	5	11-5		Jonjo O'Neill	Noel Fehily	25/1
18	4½	GEORDIE DES CHAMPS (IRE)	5	11-5		Rebecca Curtis	Leighton Aspell	100/1
19	½	JOT'EM DOWN (IRE)	5	11-5		David Bridgwater	Tom Scudamore	100/1
20	1¼	BALLYMALIN (IRE)	6	11-5		Nigel Twiston-Davies	Ryan Hatch	100/1
21	2¾	NEW TO THIS TOWN (IRE)	5	11-5		Mrs J. Harrington, Ireland	J. J. Burke	6/1
22	4	SPIRIT OF KAYF	5	11-5		Sandy Thomson	Danny Cook	100/1
23	½	WINSOME BUCKS (IRE)	6	11-5	(t)	T. Hogan, Ireland	Mr D. Queally	66/1

23 ran   Race Time 3m 47.80   Closing Sectional (3.9f): 53.2s (101.8%)   Winning Owner: Options O Syndicate

Despite a fair pace a handy position did seem something of an advantage in this year's Champion Bumper, none of the first 4 ever that far off the gallop, while Very Much So in eighth fared best of any held up early; it was still a race that tested stamina more than most bumpers, though, and it was generally a good field on looks, sure yet again to throw up several smart hurdlers/chasers and a host of future winners. **Ballyandy** was already a high achiever this season, his 3 wins including 2 strong listed events, and it barely took any further improvement to win this bigger prize, highlighting what a good jumping prospect he is though, especially given he had to make up several lengths he'd forfeited as the race was taking shape; chased leaders, shuffled back briefly 3f out, driven over 1f out, found plenty to lead final 100 yds, held on gamely; it is worth pointing out that he's a brother to Megastar, who was a similarly good bumper horse but failed to fulfil his potential over jumps, but unlike his sibling there are no signs of any quirks at all with Ballyandy at this stage. **Battleford** had obviously learnt a lot from his debut, a little green even though he won that day, and he showed much improved form to be narrowly denied a Grade 1 win just 6 weeks on; close up, went with enthusiasm, went on over 3f out, headed final 100 yds, rallied close home, just failed; he's bred to be suited by further than 2m and has all the hallmarks of one that'll make a leading novice hurdler next season. **Bacardys** won a small-field affair in the mud 12 weeks earlier, hard to assess on that evidence alone, but he coped with this much higher grade and confirmed himself a very smart jumping prospect, shaping like a stayer; chased leaders, outpaced home turn, responded well, would have benefited from a stronger gallop; he will be suited by 2½m+. **Castello Sforza** hadn't been seen since an impressive winning debut almost 12 months ago but is still very young, quite possibly just given time to mature, and he showed big improvement to be competitive, leaving the impression the experience of contesting a race like this will do him good, shaping well with that mind; tracked pace, travelled well, ran green approaching final 1f, kept on; he's an exciting prospect and one to note, both for other major bumper races this season and novice hurdles next. **Westend Story** coped with the step up in grade, showing further improvement, and was unlucky not to finish even closer; mid-division, met some trouble home turn, finished with a flourish; a good sort physically, he will prove suited by further than 2m and is one to note for novice hurdling next season. **High Bridge** backed up the improvement that he'd shown when slamming a pair of subsequent winners at Catterick 3 months ago and looked more of a threat for a long way, the stiff track just seeming to find him out late on; prominent, travelled better than most, challenged approaching final 1f, faltered final 100 yds, needs emphasis less on stamina; he's one to bear in mind for the Grade 2 at Aintree in a few weeks as that track is likely to suit him ideally. **Augusta Kate** had been seriously impressive in winning both of her previous starts in Ireland and, though a beaten, well-backed favourite, she did run well considering the hotter competition; tracked pace, ridden over 2f out, one paced; she clearly has stacks of ability but does lack size, that looking a factor here as she was buffeted around at times and seemed not to relish being crowded. **Very Much So** must have had a problem to have missed 23 months since making a winning debut but was aimed high for this belated return and put up a very useful effort in defeat, even then not seen to best effect; held up, headway 4f out but not well placed and unable to quicken; further than 2m will suit, but he's only small with jumping in mind. **First Figaro** ran well upped in grade, leaving the impression that he should have finished closer; dropped out, still plenty to do home turn, ran on, caught further back than ideal. **Rather Be** ran well upped in grade, not seen to best effect as this was run, caught a long way back, still looking rough around the edges and physically unfurnished to boot; dropped out, not settle fully, made late headway, not well placed. **Coeur Blimey** defeated Ballyandy at Ascot in mid-December but was in receipt of 4 lb that day and wasn't good enough in this even tougher race; mid-division, chased leaders 3f out, one paced. **Avenir d'Une Vie** ran creditably on form up in grade and clearly has a big engine, but not for the first time he threatened more than he delivered; tracked pace, travelled strongly, loomed up home turn, wandered final 1f, found less than looked likely; he's a well-made, chasing type in appearance. **Pride of Lecale** a compact gelding, ran about as well as could have been expected upped in grade; held up, took strong hold, crept closer out wide around 4f out, no further impression, effort proved short-lived. **Criq Rock** faced a stiff task in this grade but at least bounced back to form after a below-par effort last month (possibly needed run that day); held up, headway 3f out, met some trouble home turn, never on terms. **Turcagua** a strong gelding, might have needed the run after 16 months off, facing a stiff task in this grade, and should find the experience aiding his development; mid-division, weakened over 2f out, not knocked about. **Onthewesternfront** is a good-looker, big and strong, and although he found this too competitive, he isn't yet the finished article and should do well over jumps; raced wide, held up, some headway around 4f out, weakened over 2f out. **Compadre** was one of the better types physically (good sort) but was found out in better company, still looking rough around the edges; mid-division, lost place over 2f out, ran green, made little impression. **Geordie des Champs** looks the part, a good-topped gelding, but was simply flying too high in this grade, likely to flourish over longer trips when jumping; in rear, off the bridle before most, made no impression. **Jot'em Down** a good topped, chasing type in appearance, faced a stiff task in this grade; raced wide, held up, outpaced over 3f out, not knocked about, never on terms. **Ballymalin** was found out in better company; raced off the pace, effort around 3f out, made no impression; he's not very big (sturdy, close-coupled) which could hold him back over jumps. **New To This Town** took the eye in the paddock, a strong sort, but clearly wasn't 100% on the day; mid-division, never travelling well, lost place before halfway, beaten long way out. **Spirit of Kayf** was one of the less imposing types (leggy) and found this too competitive; soon led, headed over 3f out, soon beaten. **Winsome Bucks** is a tall, scopey sort who'll win races over jumps but was out of his depth at this level; pressed leader, folded tamely around 3f out.

CHELTENHAM Thursday March 17
GOOD

JLT Novices' Chase (Golden Miller) (Grade 1) (1) 2m 3f 198y

Pos	Btn	Horse	Age	Wgt	Eq	Trainer	Jockey	SP
1		BLACK HERCULES (IRE)	7	11-4		W. P. Mullins, Ireland	R. Walsh	4/1cf
2	3	BRISTOL DE MAI (FR)	5	11-4		Nigel Twiston-Davies	Daryl Jacob	4/1cf
3	1	L'AMI SERGE (IRE)	6	11-4		Nicky Henderson	Nico de Boinville	8/1
4	1¼	THREE MUSKETEERS (IRE)	6	11-4		Dan Skelton	Harry Skelton	8/1
5	12	AS DE MEE (FR)	6	11-4		Paul Nicholls	Sam Twiston-Davies	20/1
6	23	MOUNT GUNNERY	8	11-4		P. A. Fahy, Ireland	David Mullins	50/1
F		GARDE LA VICTOIRE (FR)	7	11-4		Philip Hobbs	Richard Johnson	4/1cf
F		OUTLANDER (IRE)	8	11-4		W. P. Mullins, Ireland	B. J. Cooper	6/1
ur		ZABANA (IRE)	7	11-4		Andrew Lynch, Ireland	Davy Russell	8/1

9 ran Race Time 4m 55.20 Closing Sectional (3.84f): 56.3s (101.2%) Winning Owner: Andrea & Graham Wylie

A Grade 1 novice, though one without the history of the Arkle or the RSA, and most of these were refugees from those 2 races, either avoiding Douvan in the Arkle, in the case of Garde La Victoire and L'Ami Serge, or giving big owners other options with their string, Outlander and Black Hercules, the latter in the same ownership as the RSA runner-up Shaneshill, both switched to this less prestigious race; the form looks no better than average for the contest, the winner running below the level achieved by Willie Mullins' previous 2 winners, Sir des Champs and Vautour, the form sure to have had more depth had Outlander and Garde La Victoire stood up 4 out, or indeed had the well-backed Zabana not been knocked out at the start; after a false start, the field was required to stand for the second start, though Zabana was moving at a angle and blocking Outlander, who bumped him, when the tape was released, the stewards' decision to find the starting procedures were followed correctly frankly hard to credit. **Black Hercules** who might have contested either the RSA or the NH Chase, was sent here instead, coping well with the drop back in trip, though likely to be at least as effective back around 3m; disputed lead until third, remained prominent, not fluent 3 out, led briefly home turn, hampered 2 out, led again run-in, kept on well; open to further improvement, though appeals more as a potential high-grade handicapper than a genuine Gold Cup prospect. **Bristol de Mai** showed further improvement, on less testing ground than previously over fences, showing a willing attitude to regain second after his jumping hadn't been so convincing as previously; led, mistake third, not fluent eighth, mistake 3 out, headed soon after, not quicken 2 out, rallied run-in; he may well have more to offer back on softer ground, also worth a try over further. **L'Ami Serge** ran well, contesting this in preference to the Arkle after his mishap at Warwick, though he left the firm impression that his stamina was stretched, even under these conditions; waited with, jumped left at times, took keen hold, headway ninth, led under pressure before 2 out, headed run-in, no extra. **Three Musketeers** ran well after 11 weeks off, quickly putting his poor effort last time behind him; held up, mistake fourth, headway tenth, effort straight, kept on run-in; he may yet have more to offer over fences, untried at 3m and likely to benefit from more emphasis on stamina than there was here, potentially a handicapper to follow in 2016/17. **As de Mee** again came up short at this level, running respectably all the same; held up, effort 3 out, mistake next, made no impression; he's yet to be tried in handicaps over fences and, given his physique, it's possible he might find a bit more at that level. **Mount Gunnery** was flying too high in this grade, soon put in his place when the principals pressed on; close up, left behind 3 out. **Garde La Victoire** beyond 2m for the first time over fences, his connections keen to avoid Douvan, was far from beaten when he departed at the top of the hill; waited with, pushed along briefly twelfth, in touch when fell next; remains open to improvement. **Outlander** might well have played a part in the finish had he not departed at the top of the hill; prominent, travelled well, yet to be asked for effort when fell 4 out; remains open to improvement. **Zabana** was bumped and unseated rider start.

Ryanair Chase (Festival) (Grade 1) (1) 2½m 166y

Pos	Btn	Horse	Age	Wgt	Eq	Trainer	Jockey	SP
1		VAUTOUR (FR)	7	11-10		W. P. Mullins, Ireland	R. Walsh	1/1f
2	6	VALSEUR LIDO (FR)	7	11-10		W. P. Mullins, Ireland	David Mullins	11/1
3	½	ROAD TO RICHES (IRE)	9	11-10		Noel Meade, Ireland	B. J. Cooper	7/1
4	1¼	AL FEROF (FR)	11	11-10		Dan Skelton	Harry Skelton	9/1
5	2¼	GILGAMBOA (IRE)	8	11-10		Enda Bolger, Ireland	Barry Geraghty	28/1
6	3¼	TAQUIN DU SEUIL (FR)	9	11-10		Jonjo O'Neill	Noel Fehily	16/1
7	7	DYNASTE (FR)	10	11-10	(b+t)	David Pipe	Tom Scudamore	20/1
8	2	JOSSES HILL (IRE)	8	11-10	(s)	Nicky Henderson	Nico de Boinville	20/1
9	3	VILLAGE VIC (IRE)	9	11-10		Philip Hobbs	Richard Johnson	20/1
10	15	OSCAR ROCK (IRE)	8	11-10	(b)	Malcolm Jefferson	Brian Hughes	66/1
11	3¼	ANNACOTTY (IRE)	8	11-10	(s)	Alan King	Ian Popham	40/1
12	6	CAPTAIN CONAN (FR)	9	11-10	(s)	Nicky Henderson	Andrew Tinkler	100/1
F		VIBRATO VALTAT (FR)	7	11-10	(t)	Paul Nicholls	Sam Twiston-Davies	33/1
pu		SMASHING (FR)	7	11-10		Henry de Bromhead, Ireland	J. J. Burke	20/1
pu		CHAMPAGNE WEST (IRE)	8	11-10		Philip Hobbs	Tom O'Brien	50/1

15 ran Race Time 5m 05.30 Closing Sectional (3.84f): 56.6s (99.8%) Winning Owner: Mrs S. Ricci

Vautour made it 3 scintillating wins from as many starts at the Cheltenham Festival 12 weeks on from his excellent second in the King George, not needing to match the form he showed then taking on this inferior set of rivals or reveal anything we didn't already know about him, but once again leaving the impression that he's potentially the best chaser in training, a point that would have been much closer to being proven one way or another had he been allowed to take his chance in the Gold Cup, which had been his stated target until the Tuesday of the Festival; always prominent and jumping well, he led going powerfully soon after 5 out, left the only remaining serious rival Road To Riches for dead on the home turn and had the race well under control in the straight, ridden out to the line for another impressive success; it's hard to see what's going to beat him in races at around this trip, and it'll be far more interesting in the future to see him back around 3m taking on the principals from the Gold Cup—another clash with the likes of Cue Card and Don Cossack, with whom he's closely matched on King George running, will be something to savour. **Valseur Lido** has blossomed into a top-class chaser and confirmed all and more of the improvement he was showing prior to departing on his last 2 starts, understandably no match for his outstanding stable companion but finishing off well to emerge a narrow best of the rest, his strength at the finish suggesting a return to 3m+ could see him in an even better light; held up, jumped soundly, headway between 5 out and 4 out, ridden next, kept on well straight, took second near finish. **Road To Riches** running in the race sponsored by his owner rather than his trainer's preferred Gold Cup, coped fine with the shorter trip and ran a cracker to finish third in top company at this meeting for the second year running, arguable even that he was second best on the day, seeming to pay the price for trying to serve it up to Vautour from 3 out, having been the only one able to go with that rival initially; close up, jumped well, went with enthusiasm, challenged 4 out, upsides home turn, no extra flat. **Al Ferof** kept fresh for this since his fine third in the King George, ran creditably back down in trip and just wasn't quite good enough against a trio of younger, Irish-trained rivals in a race that ended up taking a lot more winning than had seemed likely even in the week leading up to the Festival; mid-division, mistake fifth, in touch early final circuit, third when driven after 3 out, one paced. **Gilgamboa** without headgear this time and back down in trip, ran as well as he ever has on form without being up to the task, just falling a little short of the level required in the top open Grade 1s; mid-division, outpaced 4 out, kept on, never landed a blow, though leaving the impression he'll be worth another go at 3m this spring. **Taquin du Seuil** supplemented for this after his recent handicap win, ran creditably, quite a bit better than he had in this race last season, albeit never able to land a blow with a couple of errors not helping his cause; held up, mistakes thirteenth, 4 out, headway next, kept on. **Dynaste** winner of this race in 2014, doesn't seem the same force any longer and ran respectably judged on this season's form; held up, ridden before 5 out, made no impression. **Josses Hill** wasn't disgraced in first-time cheekpieces, jumping okay and seemingly just not good enough; chased leaders, not fluent eighth, ridden 4 out, weakened last. **Village Vic** had his winning run ended up in grade after 11 weeks off but ran better than the distance beaten suggests, trying to repeat the trailblazing tactics that have served him well at a lower level but finding them much harder to pull off, paying the price for that late on; made running, mistake eleventh, headed after 5 out, ridden when mistake 3 out, weakened last. **Oscar Rock** after 4 months off, was out of depth; in rear, struggling long way out. **Annacotty** has done well in handicaps here this season but found this much too competitive; mid-division, struggling badly tenth. **Captain Conan** faced a stiff task mindful of how little he'd shown in 2 recent runs and was well held in first-time cheekpieces; always behind. **Vibrato Valtat** upped in trip after 8 weeks off, failed to complete, though ran as if in good nick; held up, headway in ninth when fell 4 out, a bit too far out to be sure exactly how he'd have fared. **Smashing** had winning run ended, finding this much tougher, and though he ran okay up to a point late mistakes took their toll; prominent, mistakes eleventh, 5 out and 4 out, not fluent again 3 out, weakened. **Champagne West** had plenty to find but ran especially badly, as though a recent fall had left its mark; in rear, never travelling well, beaten long way out.

Ryanair World Hurdle (Grade 1) (1) 2m 7f 213y

Pos	Btn	Horse	Age	Wgt	Eq	Trainer	Jockey	SP
1		THISTLECRACK	8	11-10		Colin Tizzard	Tom Scudamore	1/1f
2	7	ALPHA DES OBEAUX (FR)	6	11-10		M. F. Morris, Ireland	B. J. Cooper	8/1
3	22	BOBS WORTH (IRE)	11	11-10		Nicky Henderson	David Bass	33/1
4	1¾	COLE HARDEN (IRE)	7	11-10	(t)	Warren Greatrex	Gavin Sheehan	15/2
5	9	AUX PTITS SOINS (FR)	6	11-10		Paul Nicholls	Nick Scholfield	16/1
6	4½	SAPHIR DU RHEU (FR)	7	11-10		Paul Nicholls	Sam Twiston-Davies	11/1
7	¾	MARTELLO TOWER (IRE)	8	11-10		Mrs Margaret Mullins, Ireland	A. P. Heskin	14/1
8	¾	WHISPER (FR)	8	11-10		Nicky Henderson	Nico de Boinville	9/1
pu		KNOCKARA BEAU (IRE)	13	11-10		George Charlton	Liam Treadwell	100/1
pu		AT FISHERS CROSS (IRE)	9	11-10	(b)	Rebecca Curtis	Barry Geraghty	33/1
pu		KILCOOLEY (IRE)	7	11-10	(t)	Charlie Longsdon	Richard Johnson	20/1
pu		LIEUTENANT COLONEL	7	11-10	(t)	Ms Sandra Hughes, Ireland	Davy Russell	33/1

12 ran Race Time 5m 42.00 Closing Sectional (7.1f): 98.4s (102.9%) Winning Owner: John and Heather Snook

A representative field of stayers was put to the sword by the season's dominant performer in this division, Thistlecrack, who won more decisively than any had done in this race this century and produced a performance right up there with the best that Big Buck's or Baracouda managed in the Stayers/World Hurdle; the pace was good enough to ensure a thorough test of stamina, more so than is sometimes the case in this race, those who tried to get the winner in trouble paying for their exertions. **Thistlecrack** had dominated this division all winter and demolished his rivals with a nigh-on perfect display, producing as good a performance in this race as even Big Buck's and Baracouda managed; waited with, jumped well, tanked along, went prominent halfway, led 2 out, stayed on strongly straight, impressive; he is reportedly being considered for a novice chase campaign, ending in the Gold Cup, which makes sense, given his age, though he's so good at this discipline that it's hard to see what would trouble him were he to be kept to hurdling. **Alpha des Obeaux** was better than ever, showing form more than good enough to have won an average running of this race, just no match for an outstanding winner; in touch, travelled well, headway before 3 out, chased leader next, kept on well, no impression on winner; his best chance of a win at this level may well come at Punchestown, but fences surely beckon next season, and he's an exciting prospect who should take high rank among the staying novices. **Bobs Worth** ran much better than when last seen to reach a place, for all that he was possibly flattered in picking up the pieces late on, and this would be a fitting way to end his career, the scene of his greatest triumphs, the winner of 3 Grade 1 events at the Festival, including the 2013 Gold Cup; close up, mistake seventh, not quicken 3 out, rallied well straight, took third run-in. **Cole Harden** was back on less testing ground but failed to better his last run after 11 weeks off, again well below his best for all this was an altogether stronger renewal of the race than the one he landed in 2015; led, pushed along after 3 out, headed 2 out, weakened straight. **Aux Ptits Soins** upped in trip on his first start since winning last season's Coral Cup, shaped encouragingly up in grade, either short of stamina or fitness, showing enough to think he will be competitive at this level, the Aintree Hurdle perhaps an option next time; in rear, travelled well, headway 3 out, took third straight, weakened late on; remains capable of better. **Saphir du Rheu** kept over hurdles after 3 months off, was easy to back and just wasn't in the same form as when runner-up to Cole Harden in 2015, questions to answer whether he stays hurdling or goes back chasing next, even remembering how good he was over fences at Aintree last spring;

prominent, ridden before 3 out, weakening when mistake next. **Martello Tower** on less testing ground, was well below form; prominent, pushed along ninth, left behind 2 out. **Whisper** couldn't be fancied on his 2 previous efforts this season and duly finished well held after 11 weeks off, not seeing his race out; waited with, mistake eighth, ridden after, weakened 2 out; his record over the last couple of seasons suggest he's not easy to train. **Knockara Beau** found this all too much at this late stage of his career; disputed lead until third, lost place next, tailed off halfway, pulled up straight. **At Fishers Cross** had made the frame in the last 2 runnings of this but ran no sort of race on this occasion; raced off the pace, made mistakes, labouring after halfway, pulled up before 3 out. **Kilcooley** ran poorly after 5 months off, his preparation for this reportedly not ideal, though for his 2 standout efforts he very much had things go his way and he might struggle to reproduce the form anyway; prominent, took keen hold, disputed lead long way out, struggling when bad mistake 3 out, pulled up. **Lieutenant Colonel** was ridden much more patiently than usual but it failed to make any difference, just outclassed; dropped out, ridden eighth, behind when all but unseated rider 3 out, pulled up.

CHELTENHAM Friday March 18
GOOD

JCB Triumph Hurdle (Grade 1) (1) 2m 179y

Pos	Btn	Horse	Age	Wgt	Eq	Trainer	Jockey	SP
1		IVANOVICH GORBATOV (IRE)	4	11-0	(t)	Aidan O'Brien, Ireland	Barry Geraghty	9/2f
2	1¼	APPLE'S JADE (FR)	4	10-7		W. P. Mullins, Ireland	B. J. Cooper	12/1
3	6	FOOTPAD (FR)	4	11-0	(h)	W. P. Mullins, Ireland	R. Walsh	5/1
4	7	LET'S DANCE (FR)	4	10-7		W. P. Mullins, Ireland	P. Townend	11/1
5	nk	LEONCAVALLO (IRE)	4	11-0		John Ferguson	Aidan Coleman	18/1
6	½	CLAN DES OBEAUX (FR)	4	11-0		Paul Nicholls	Noel Fehily	12/1
7	½	TOMMY SILVER (FR)	4	11-0		Paul Nicholls	J. J. Burke	25/1
8	1¼	FRODON (FR)	4	11-0		Paul Nicholls	Sean Bowen	20/1
9	2¾	GIBRALFARO (IRE)	4	11-0	(s)	Alan King	Wayne Hutchinson	25/1
10	4	CONSUL DE THAIX (FR)	4	11-0		Nicky Henderson	Mark Walsh	33/1
11	½	CONNETABLE (FR)	4	11-0	(s)	Paul Nicholls	Sam Twiston-Davies	14/1
12	1	SCEAU ROYAL (FR)	4	11-0		Alan King	Daryl Jacob	8/1
13	7	ZUBAYR (IRE)	4	11-0		Paul Nicholls	Nick Scholfield	11/2
14	10	WHO DARES WINS (IRE)	4	11-0		Alan King	Richard Johnson	10/1
15	ds	BIG MCINTOSH (IRE)	4	11-0		John Ryan	Mattie Batchelor	150/1

15 ran Race Time 3m 55.00 Closing Sectional (7.10f): 97.70s (101.6%) Winning Owner: Mr John P. McManus

This looked a competitive Triumph Hurdle rather than a strong one, nothing in the division having set the bar that high up to this point; this is often the stage for the best performances, however, and the first 2 both showed plenty of improvement, Ivanovich Gorbatov running to a level only slightly below the 5-year average for the race; Big McIntosh raced clear but was largely ignored and the pace certainly wasn't too strong, Footpad faring best of those who were out the back. **Ivanovich Gorbatov** had disappointed behind a couple of these rivals at Leopardstown 6 weeks earlier but no doubt this was the main target all along, whilst less testing conditions were a positive for him too (impressive winner of Flat handicap on good ground last summer), and he showed plenty of improvement to live up to his big reputation, value for more than the winning margin; mid-division, tanked along and jumped well, went handy 2 out, ridden with loads of confidence and loomed up approaching last, shaken up and quickened to lead final 100 yds, well on top at the finish; he's a high-class prospect and will be hard to beat if sent to Aintree and/or Punchestown for the other juvenile Grade 1s. **Apple's Jade** is most progressive and built on the excellent impression she'd created when winning a Grade 2 on her debut for Willie Mullins in December, confirming superiority over Footpad from that day, less testing ground no problem for her; prominent, jumped accurately, went with enthusiasm, led after 3 out, pressed on between last 2, headed final 100 yds, kept on; she remains with potential and is nailed on to win more good races, with mares contests open to her as well, also likely to stay 2½m which will increase options. **Footpad** may not have confirmed superiority over Ivanovich Gorbatov under these less testing conditions but, in form terms, he backed up that previous effort; dropped out, still plenty to do 3 out, good progress between last 2, kept on; he's proved consistent and versatile in this first season. **Let's Dance** ran creditably, not far below the form she'd shown when third to Footpad at Leopardstown, simply not quick enough or good enough to match the first 3; chased leaders, close up 2 out, one paced from home turn; she's worth a try at around 2½m and will no doubt be a force in mares graded events, still open to improvement. **Leoncavallo** wasn't disgraced after 3 months off in what was by some way the hottest race he's been involved in; held up, untidy 2 out, headway before last, one paced; he's presumably been freshened up with a spring campaign in mind and ought to give a good account in the Grade 1 at Aintree, where the flat track might suit him ideally. **Clan des Obeaux** wasn't seen to best effect on ground less testing than he'd raced on previously in Britain; chased leaders, hit 4 out, outpaced after 2 out, held when not fluent last, plugged on, needs emphasis more on stamina; he remains with potential, likely to flourish next season. **Tommy Silver** ran about as well as could have been expected upped in grade and should find this aiding his development; held up, pushed along after fifth, late headway without threatening. **Frodon** was found out in better company, running to a similar level of form as when winning small-field affair at Haydock last time; mid-division, ridden after 2 out, weakened, not knocked about. **Gibralfaro** in first-time cheekpieces, again ran below form and seems to have gone off the boil after winning his first 2 starts in this sphere; raced wide, held up, in touch after third, weakened between last 2. **Consul de Thaix** faced a stiff task in this grade and isn't yet the finished article; held up, some headway between 3 out and 2 out, effort flattened out, not unduly punished; still unexposed. **Connetable** in first-time cheekpieces, produced a laboured effort on ground less testing than he'd encountered on previous British starts; raced off the pace, off the bridle before most, never on terms. **Sceau Royal** disappointed after 9 weeks off but it's his first below-par run of the season to be fair; mid-division, effort after 2 out, tied up. **Zubayr** looked a smart prospect when winning the Adonis and, though that form might not be worth as much as it seemed at the time, he clearly failed to give his running here and is worth another chance; mid-division, took keen hold, struggling 2 out. **Who Dares Wins** clearly wasn't 100% on the day; chased leaders, weakened 2 out, not persevered with once held. **Big McIntosh** after 4 months off, was flying too high in this grade; raced clear, typically took strong hold, headed after 3 out, folded.

Albert Bartlett Novices' Hurdle (Spa) (Grade 1) (1) 2m 7f 213y

Pos	Btn	Horse	Age	Wgt	Eq	Trainer	Jockey	SP
1		UNOWHATIMEANHARRY	8	11-5	(t)	Harry Fry	Noel Fehily	11/1
2	1¼	FAGAN	6	11-5		Gordon Elliott, Ireland	Davy Russell	33/1
3	1½	CHAMPERS ON ICE (IRE)	6	11-5	(s)	David Pipe	Tom Scudamore	20/1
4	1¾	BARTERS HILL (IRE)	6	11-5		Ben Pauling	David Bass	4/1
5	11	BALKO DES FLOS (FR)	5	11-5		W. P. Mullins, Ireland	David Mullins	40/1
6	7	ALLYSSON MONTERG (FR)	6	11-5		Richard Hobson	Alain Cawley	40/1
7	6	GANGSTER (FR)	6	11-5		W. P. Mullins, Ireland	B. J. Cooper	15/2
8	8	OPEN EAGLE (IRE)	7	11-5		W. P. Mullins, Ireland	M. P. Fogarty	20/1
9	3¼	JONNIESOFA (IRE)	6	11-5		Rose Dobbin	Craig Nichol	40/1
10	hd	AURILLAC (FR)	6	11-5		Rebecca Curtis	Nico de Boinville	33/1
11	10	WEST APPROACH	6	11-5		Colin Tizzard	Aidan Coleman	66/1
F		BLEU ET ROUGE (FR)	5	11-5		W. P. Mullins, Ireland	Barry Geraghty	10/1
ur		LONG DOG	6	11-5		W. P. Mullins, Ireland	R. Walsh	5/1
ur		BACHASSON (FR)	5	11-5		W. P. Mullins, Ireland	Mr P. W. Mullins	28/1
pu		UP FOR REVIEW (IRE)	7	11-5		W. P. Mullins, Ireland	P. Townend	12/1
pu		ATLANTIC GOLD (IRE)	6	11-5		Charlie Longsdon	Brian Hughes	100/1
pu		DEFINITE OUTCOME (IRE)	7	11-5		Rebecca Curtis	J. J. Burke	66/1
pu		SHANTOU VILLAGE (IRE)	6	11-5		Neil Mulholland	Richard Johnson	7/2f
pu		HIT THE HIGHWAY (IRE)	7	11-5		Giles Smyly	Tom Cannon	100/1

19 ran Race Time 5m 48.10 Closing Sectional (7.10f): 101.00s (102.1%) Winning Owner: Harry Fry Racing Club

A race that often attracts a large field and that was certainly the case this year, 19 of them lining up, indicative perhaps of an open division, the standard-setting Barters Hill not without questions to answer in a tough environment like this, and with him failing to quite match his previous efforts and the well-backed favourite Shantou Village having a problem on the day, it took less winning than it might have done; the pace was contested and fairly strong, Unowhatimeanharry and Fagan perhaps helped to some extent by more patient rides than the third/fourth. **Unowhatimeanharry** is one of the success stories of the season, a huge improver since joining Harry Fry from Helen Nelmes, the winner of a handicap from a BHA mark of 123 at the Open meeting here in November, unbeaten since taking in 2 more handicaps, a Grade 2 and now this premier staying novice; held up, steady headway after 3 out, ridden next, stayed on to lead last, untidy there, hung right, driven out; he'll reportedly miss Aintree and be aimed at Punchestown, understandably so having had a hard race here. **Fagan** had his stamina really tested for the first time and that brought about significant improvement as he almost caused a big surprise up in grade, proving himself a smart, highly-progressive novice hurdler, and he's an exciting prospect for chasing, a rangy sort who won 3 points in 2015; raced wide, patiently ridden, headway under pressure after 2 out, stayed on strongly, suited by emphasis on stamina; he's still totally unexposed as a stayer. **Champers On Ice** ran a personal best to be placed at Grade 1 level, suited by the 3f longer trip and maybe benefiting from first-time cheekpieces too, and given that he was beaten only by a pair much more patiently ridden he perhaps deserves some extra credit; chased leaders, went with enthusiasm, hit seventh, ninth, edged ahead after 2 out, headed approaching last, one paced; he looks every inch a chaser and is one to look forward to over fences next season. **Barters Hill** lost his unbeaten record in a much more competitive race than those he'd contested over hurdles previously, up against only 2 rivals when he won the Challow of course, but it was a creditable effort, especially as he did plenty towards the head of affairs, plus he was reported to have not had the ideal preparation—apparently stiff in his box a couple of days earlier—and all in all he's well worth another chance in one of the other top staying novice hurdles this spring, be it at Aintree (won Grade 2 bumper there last year) or Punchestown; close up, led third, pushed along after ninth, headed after 2 out, led again before last, headed again there, hung left, no extra, possibly did too much too soon; he does have the look of a chaser and next season going over fences would appeal as a better option that contesting some of the top hurdle races. **Balko des Flos** ran well upped in grade, showing improvement, and that's despite not totally convincing with his stamina for the 4f longer trip, looking more threatening for a long way; raced wide, held up, travelled well, crept closer after sixth, chased leaders ninth, one paced from 2 out; may prove best at shorter than 3m and remains open to improvement. **Allysson Monterg** had no problem with the 4f longer trip, class rather than stamina the reason for him dropping back after the second last, and he ran about as well as could have been expected at this level; prominent, not fluent 3 out, faded between last 2; still lightly raced and probably has more to offer back in calmer waters. **Gangster** had reportedly suffered a slight setback after winning at Fairyhouse before Christmas and shaped as if needing the run after 3 months off (also lost a shoe which might have contributed to a weak finish); mid-division, travelled better than most, went handy after 3 out, found less than looked likely, not unduly punished. **Open Eagle** failed to stay 3f longer trip, shaped as if still in good form; held up, travelled well, hit seventh, headway after 3 out, weakened, found the test too much; likely to prove best up to 21f. **Jonniesofa** better judged on previous form, possibly unsuited by conditions (all wins have been on heavy ground); chased leaders, ridden after 3 out, left behind approaching next. **Aurillac** found this too competitive; raced wide, in touch, went in snatches, weakened after 3 out; should stay further than 19f, although possibly doesn't want this far (not bred for 3m). **West Approach** was out of depth; raced wide, mid-division, not settle fully, weakening when mistake 3 out. **Bleu Et Rouge** failed to complete, out of the race before stamina for the markedly longer trip (up 6f) came into play; mid-field, fell eighth, too far out to suggest outcome. **Long Dog** mid-division, went wrong after fourth, fatally injured. **Bachasson** was surprisingly hiked right up in trip, never having shaped like a stayer, but was given a very patient ride to give him the best chance of getting home and looked set to finish fifth when unseating at the final flight; dropped out, went with enthusiasm, blundered third, headway after 3 out, held but keeping on when unseated rider last, would have run respectably. **Up For Review** clearly wasn't 100% on the day; typically took strong hold, led until third, remained prominent, folded tamely after 3 out, seemed amiss. **Atlantic Gold** was well held after 3 months off, not up to the task; raced wide, close up, lost place after ninth, soon done with. **Definite Outcome** faced a stiff task but clearly wasn't 100% on the day, anyway; tracked pace, blundered seventh, struggling badly next. **Shantou Village** was beaten by more than lack of stamina over 3f longer trip, clearly amiss, the vet reporting afterwards that he'd been struck into on his left hind; held up, headway 3 out, shaken up before next, found nothing, heavily eased off; it's worth pointing out that he'd twice beaten the third comfortably earlier in the season, so his form is strong. **Hit The Highway** shaped as if amiss, possibly unsuited by conditions that were much less testing than for his wins; mid-division, lost place sixth, beaten long way out.

Timico Cheltenham Gold Cup Chase (Grade 1) (1) 3¼m 70y

Pos	Btn	Horse	Age	Wgt	Eq	Trainer	Jockey	SP
1		DON COSSACK (GER)	9	11-10	(t)	Gordon Elliott, Ireland	B. J. Cooper	9/4f
2	4½	DJAKADAM (FR)	7	11-10		W. P. Mullins, Ireland	R. Walsh	9/2
3	10	DON POLI (IRE)	7	11-10		W. P. Mullins, Ireland	Davy Russell	9/2
4	7	CARLINGFORD LOUGH (IRE)	10	11-10		John E. Kiely, Ireland	Barry Geraghty	25/1
5	ns	IRISH CAVALIER (IRE)	7	11-10	(s)	Rebecca Curtis	P. Townend	66/1
6	16	SMAD PLACE (FR)	9	11-10		Alan King	Wayne Hutchinson	10/1
7	15	O'FAOLAINS BOY (IRE)	9	11-10	(s)	Rebecca Curtis	Noel Fehily	40/1
8	1½	ON HIS OWN (IRE)	12	11-10	(s)	W. P. Mullins, Ireland	Mr P. W. Mullins	50/1
F		CUE CARD	10	11-10	(t)	Colin Tizzard	Paddy Brennan	5/2

9 ran Race Time 6m 33.30 Closing Sectional (3.84f): 57.40s (100.0%) Winning Owner: Gigginstown House Stud

Only once this century—Bobs Worth's year in 2013—has the Gold Cup attracted so few runners, but any numerical shortfall was more than compensated by a near-stellar line-up missing only long-since injured reigning champion Coneygree and the previous day's Ryanair winner Vautour, the current holders of the Hennessy, King George and Lexus all in attendance, not to mention last year's runner-up, providing context to another bona fide top-notch performance by Don Cossack, cementing his status as the best chaser in training; there was a contested pace—if not so searching as last year's—that lifted again from 5 out, though the main players had still to reveal their hands when Cue Card crashed out at the third last, robbing the British challenge of its only realistic contender, the unknown as to how he'd have fared the only slight on an otherwise fair and representative renewal. **Don Cossack** underlined his brilliance as he made amends for his King George spill and earlier miscues at this track, in a role reversal from Kempton proving the beneficiary of Cue Card's fall just as the race was developing, still left with a top-class Djakadam to fend off and making doing so look all rather routine, no dramas at all save for a slight peck 4 out as his effort was starting, sent on by Cooper entering the straight and requiring little more than riding out, even with the runner-up seeing things out as strongly as he had 12 months earlier; he'll be the one to beat in all the top staying races again next season, but the small matter of defending his Aintree and Punchestown crowns awaits more immediately. **Djakadam** had to settle for second in this for the second successive season but would have won many a more ordinary renewal with either effort, running into a freak novice in Coneygree last year and the best stayer around this, closing the gap with the winner from their meeting at Punchestown but not by enough; soon travelling with his trademark purpose, with no sign at all of the jumping blemishes that had ended his 2 other visits to Cheltenham, he moved upsides between 4 out and 3 out and stuck to his task doggedly even after Don Cossack had put him away on the home turn, emerging with great credit; he's young enough to remain a fixture for another few years yet. **Don Poli** is probably only fifth or so in the current staying pecking order in any case but would have benefited from more positive tactics—and likely softer ground—on the day, not seeming so idle as often but caught out of his ground as the pace lifted, all too late by the time he properly got going, taking third at the last with the front pair long since away; he's still to be tried in headgear by current trainer, a prime candidate if ever there was one. **Carlingford Lough** ran much as he had at Leopardstown 6 weeks earlier but his late surge from an unpromising position wasn't anything like so potent in this far stronger Grade 1, running as well as could be expected on form as he edged fourth on the line having still been well back 3 out; he's more than ready for long distances now. **Irish Cavalier** seemed to excel himself in the face of a hopeless task but probably benefited from biding his time in a well-run race, even then not lasting out the longer trip, sweeping into fourth past the 2 front-runners between the last 2 only to fade on the run-in, edged out for a frame finish on the line. **Smad Place** failed to do himself justice in this for the second year in a row, unable to get into the same rhythm away from the mud with O'Faolains Boy taking him on in front, struggling to hold his place alongside the big guns well before that rival (left behind before 4 out) and ending up a place ahead only after that horse wilted in the straight. **O'Faolains Boy** shaped much better than the bare result in first-time cheekpieces but paid the price for the boldness of his tactics in a race he couldn't realistically win, jumping/travelling well and seeing off Smad Place in their private battle from the sixteenth only to tie up badly from 3 out, having been in front from the sixteenth to before 4 out. **On His Own** wasn't asked/able to lead and ran another of his moody races, losing his place before the seventh and struggling some way out. **Cue Card** was robbed of his chance of another fairytale win by a rare jumping lapse 3 out, only his second ever spill over fences, coming just as he'd moved upsides, still going powerfully at the time but with niggling stamina questions still to answer, odds against he'd have been able to withstand Don Cossack even if he'd got home, though second (rated as such) would have been a perfectly creditable finish; he's a different horse now to the one hammered by Don Cossack at Aintree last spring, but he's still likely to play second fiddle if the pair meet there again.

AINTREE Thursday April 7
Mildmay & National courses: GOOD to SOFT, Hurdles course: SOFT

Betfred Bowl Chase (Grade 1) (1) 3m 210y

Pos	Btn	Horse	Age	Wgt	Eq	Trainer	Jockey	SP
1		CUE CARD	10	11-7	(t)	Colin Tizzard	Paddy Brennan	6/5f
2	9	DON POLI (IRE)	7	11-7		W. P. Mullins, Ireland	B. J. Cooper	4/1
3	8	DJAKADAM (FR)	7	11-7		W. P. Mullins, Ireland	R. Walsh	5/2
4	5	DYNASTE (FR)	10	11-7	(b+t)	David Pipe	Tom Scudamore	33/1
5	6	TAQUIN DU SEUIL (FR)	9	11-7		Jonjo O'Neill	Noel Fehily	22/1
6	16	SAPHIR DU RHEU (FR)	7	11-7		Paul Nicholls	Sam Twiston-Davies	12/1
F		IRISH CAVALIER (IRE)	7	11-7	(b)	Rebecca Curtis	P. Townend	25/1
pu		HOUBLON DES OBEAUX (FR)	9	11-7	(s)	Venetia Williams	Aidan Coleman	33/1
pu		WAKANDA (IRE)	7	11-7		Sue Smith	Danny Cook	50/1

9 ran Race Time 6m 41.20 Closing Sectional (3.15f): 51.5s (98.4%) Winning Owner: Mrs Jean R. Bishop

Even without Don Cossack this was a fantastic renewal of the Bowl, involving 3 of the other Grade 1 staying-chase winners this season in Cue Card, Don Poli and Djakadam, and that trio dominated from some way out in a well-run affair that got them well strung out. **Cue Card** quickly gained compensation for what might have been in the Gold Cup and capped off what has been a brilliant season, his third Grade 1 success of the campaign adding to the Betfair and King George, and this was the most emphatic of the lot; in touch, typically travelled strongly, mistakes sixth, ninth, loomed up 4 out, jumped on 3 out, in command between last 2, eased off towards finish and was most impressive; he could head to Punchestown in a few weeks for what would be a mouthwatering rematch with Don Cossack. **Don Poli** isn't quite in the same league as the likes of Cue Card and Don Cossack, that exposed both in the Gold Cup and here, but that pair are truly elite staying chasers and this was another top-class performance to be clear second best on the day; prominent, jumped well, shaken up after fourteenth, upsides 3 out, kept on but no match for winner; he's overdue praise for how he's held his form not just this season but all the way through his career, Punchestown last spring literally his only blip, and he's nailed on to remain competitive in these top 3m+ races for a good while yet. **Djakadam** ran a huge race in the Gold Cup less than 3 weeks ago and it had seemingly taken more out of him than it had his stablemate, Don Poli, lacking the same verve here and finishing quite tired; close up, led fourth, hit twelfth, headed 3 out, held when pecked last, no extra; he'll benefit from a break rather than going to Punchestown. **Dynaste** struggles to be truly competitive at this level nowadays, not the force he was a couple of years ago, but at least this was one of his better efforts of the season, despite an unusual situation when hit by a broken rail (gave way due to photographer leaning on it) early on; led early, headed fourth, outpaced fourteenth, plugged on, no match for principals. **Taquin du Seuil** simply wasn't up to the task, no shame up against some of the best chasers around; dropped out, crept closer tenth, outpaced thirteenth, never landed a blow. **Saphir du Rheu** has had a disappointing season overall, operating way below his best at present, albeit in the heat of this race for longer than most; chased leaders, slow eleventh, hit 4 out, weakened before next; he does have something to prove at present. **Irish Cavalier** in first-time blinkers, was in the process of running creditably when departing late on; held up, headway fourteenth, keeping on in fourth when fell last (a couple of lengths ahead of Dynaste at the time). **Houblon des Obeaux** ran no sort of race on less testing ground than ideal; took little interest, jumped sketchily, pulled up after eleventh. **Wakanda** was flying too high in this grade; chased leaders, lost place fourth, mistake twelfth, soon done with.

Doom Bar Aintree Hurdle (Grade 1) (1) 2½m

Pos	Btn	Horse	Age	Wgt	Eq	Trainer	Jockey	SP
1		ANNIE POWER (IRE)	8	11-0		W. P. Mullins, Ireland	R. Walsh	4/9f
2	18	MY TENT OR YOURS (IRE)	9	11-7	(h)	Nicky Henderson	Barry Geraghty	9/1
3	9	NICHOLS CANYON	6	11-7		W. P. Mullins, Ireland	P. Townend	11/2
4	21	COURT MINSTREL (IRE)	9	11-7		Evan Williams	Paul Moloney	100/1
5	42	CAMPING GROUND (FR)	6	11-7	(t)	Robert Walford	Leighton Aspell	20/1
F		THE NEW ONE (IRE)	8	11-7		Nigel Twiston-Davies	Sam Twiston-Davies	8/1

6 ran Race Time 5m 06.20 Closing Sectional (3.20f): 49.8s (98.4%) Winning Owner: Mrs S. Ricci

Less a race than a coronation, Annie Power's clear-cut success cementing her status as the leading shorter-distance hurdler around in the injury-enforced absence of stablemate Faugheen, even a sensibly conservative view of the bare form—the 3 Champion Hurdle frame-fillers who reopposed either failed to complete or clearly failed to perform—putting her in advance of fellow Mullins-trained Arctic Fire in the hurdling hierarchy. **Annie Power** would give an on-song Faugheen all he could handle in receipt of her mares allowance, making the trio she'd already hammered in the Champion Hurdle easy prey again here, a cut above on these terms even if The New One's fall and the clearly below-par efforts of the placed pair from Cheltenham exaggerated her superiority, taking over around halfway and sauntering clear from 3 out as the second/third wilted, testament to her durability and versatility that she'd be able to perform at 100% over a different trip just 3 weeks on while her main rivals weren't; she'll continue to take all the beating and, having not returned to the track until mid-February, she'll be fresher than most who attempt a Cheltenham, Aintree and Punchestown triple-header, last achieved outside hunter company by Sprinter Sacre in 2013. **My Tent Or Yours** wouldn't have beaten Annie Power at 2m but certainly left the impression he didn't stay the longer trip on a belated first try, the quick turnaround—having been off so long prior to Cheltenham—another possible explanation for his feeble finishing effort, typically taking a strong hold yet seemingly going well when moved close up 3 out only to wilt from the next. **Nichols Canyon** has yet to finish out of the placings when completing but his 2 runs either side of Cheltenham have been undeniably tame, looking ill at ease from early on here (jumped right and lost lead over a circuit out) before folding badly in the straight. **Court Minstrel** was out of his depth after 11 weeks off but picked up in excess of £10,000 for turning up, making no impression whilst not subjected to an unduly hard race. **Camping Ground** should have been suited by the return to further but ran even worse than when put in his place in the Champion Hurdle, dropping away in strides at the end of the back straight; he's either flattered by his win in the Relkeel or else left his season behind in producing that career-best display. **The New One** survived one mistake at the third only to fall heavily 2 flights later; this was his first ever non-completion, but that shouldn't mask the fact his jumping has long since been a weakness.

AINTREE Friday April 8
GOOD to SOFT

Imagine Cruising First In The Frame Top Novices' Hurdle (Grade 1) (1) 2m 103y

Pos	Btn	Horse	Age	Wgt	Eq	Trainer	Jockey	SP
1		BUVEUR D'AIR (FR)	5	11-4		Nicky Henderson	Noel Fehily	11/4
2	nk	PETIT MOUCHOIR (FR)	5	11-4		W. P. Mullins, Ireland	David Mullins	40/1
3	8	LIMINI (IRE)	5	10-11		W. P. Mullins, Ireland	R. Walsh	11/10f
4	¾	NORTH HILL HARVEY	5	11-4		Dan Skelton	Harry Skelton	25/1
5	¾	BLEU ET ROUGE (FR)	5	11-4		W. P. Mullins, Ireland	Barry Geraghty	8/1
6	½	AGRAPART (FR)	5	11-4		Nick Williams	Lizzie Kelly	10/1
7	2¼	BALL D'ARC (FR)	5	11-4		Gordon Elliott, Ireland	B. J. Cooper	16/1
8	26	THREE STARS (IRE)	6	11-4		Henry de Bromhead, Ireland	J. J. Burke	50/1
ur		ALTRUISM (IRE)	6	11-4	(h)	James Moffatt	Brian Hughes	100/1
ur		GWAFA (IRE)	5	11-4		Paul Webber	Richie McLernon	16/1
pu		MARRACUDJA (FR)	5	11-4	(h+t)	Paul Nicholls	Sam Twiston-Davies	50/1

11 ran   Race Time 4m 04.50   Closing Sectional (3.2f): 46.9s (101.3%)   Winning Owner: Potensis Bloodstock Ltd & Chris Giles

With Limini not performing to the same level as she had at Cheltenham this took a bit less winning than perhaps seemed likely, not that the form shown by the winner is significantly below the usual standard for the race; the pace was nothing out of the ordinary, the runner-up helped to some degree by being close up throughout, though rather than thinking he's flattered in any way it's simply worth giving Buveur d'Air a bit of extra credit for pegging him back. **Buveur d'Air** didn't need to improve with Limini underperforming but his efforts both here and in the Supreme confirm that he's a highly promising young hurdler and he showed a lot of likeable attributes to get this done, value for a bit extra than the neck he won by; mid-division, travelled well, crept closer after 4 out, close up next, upsides last, kept on well, edged ahead close home and showed a good attitude; he'll probably stay 2½m and seems sure to do better still next season. **Petit Mouchoir** without the headgear this time, showed much improved form, proving that he can cut it at this level after all, a really smart effort to push Buveur d'Air all the way to the line even if well positioned; pressed leader, went with enthusiasm, went on after 4 out, shaken up after next, stayed on, edged out only late on and pulled clear of remainder; he's quite an exuberant type and perhaps a flat track like this is ideal. **Limini** is a lot better than this, as her impressive Cheltenham performance highlights, and there were excuses for not matching it, too lit up to see things out fully; mid-division, raced too freely, tracked pace 3 out, hit next, one paced; better judged on what's gone before and remains capable of better. **North Hill Harvey** wasn't up to the task kept to Grade 1 company but ran well, close to his best previous form; held up, headway 3 out, one paced from next; he's still young and lightly raced and has promised even more at times, including for a long way in the Supreme, and he could be the sort to win a valuable handicap or 2 in the future. **Bleu Et Rouge** who'd fallen before the race began in earnest in the Albert Bartlett 3 weeks earlier, was back down markedly in trip and ran respectably without the race getting right to the bottom of him; mid-division, not settle fully, crept closer 3 out, chased leaders next, one paced, not unduly punished; he's worth a try at 2½m. **Agrapart** wasn't disgraced back in Grade 1 company but seemed laboured in comparison to when winning the Betfair Hurdle 2 months ago, the less testing ground probably not ideal given how well he handles the mud; tracked pace, off the bridle long way out, close up 3 out, hit next, one paced. **Ball d'Arc** ran respectably and was just found out in better company having won relatively uncompetitive listed/Grade 2 events in Ireland earlier in the season; held up, headway out wide before 3 out, effort flattened out; he's a winning pointer and his future probably lies over fences. **Three Stars** was well held after 5 months off, faced with a stiff task in this grade; raced wide, chased leaders, ridden when mistake 3 out, weakened, behind when flattened last. **Altruism** in a first-time hood, failed to complete; tracked pace, unseated rider fourth, too far out to suggest outcome. **Gwafa** failed to complete through no fault of his own, mid-division when badly hampered and unseated at the fourth; he remains with potential. **Marracudja** clearly wasn't 100% on the day; led, headed after sixth, struggling badly before 3 out, eased and was pulled up before last.

Betfred Mildmay Novices' Chase (Grade 1) (1) 3m 210y

Pos	Btn	Horse	Age	Wgt	Eq	Trainer	Jockey	SP
1		NATIVE RIVER (IRE)	6	11-4	(s)	Colin Tizzard	Richard Johnson	11/2
2	3	HENRI PARRY MORGAN	8	11-4	(s+t)	Peter Bowen	Sean Bowen	10/1
3	3¾	BLAKLION	7	11-4		Nigel Twiston-Davies	Ryan Hatch	3/1
4	7	UN TEMPS POUR TOUT (IRE)	7	11-4	(b+t)	David Pipe	Tom Scudamore	6/4f
5	8	BALLYALTON (IRE)	9	11-4	(s)	Ian Williams	Brian Hughes	20/1
6	21	ROI DES FRANCS (FR)	7	11-4	(h)	W. P. Mullins, Ireland	B. J. Cooper	10/1
7	15	OUT SAM	7	11-4		Warren Greatrex	Gavin Sheehan	16/1
pu		OTAGO TRAIL (IRE)	8	11-4		Venetia Williams	Aidan Coleman	20/1

8 ran Race Time 6m 27.60 Closing Sectional (3.15f): 49.2s (99.5%) Winning Owner: Brocade Racing

A hole has rather been left in this season's staying novice chase scene with the physical problems of More of That and the ill-fated No More Heroes, with that pair having looked the most exciting in the division mid-season, and it's representative of this point that, just like the RSA at Cheltenham, this form is rated quite a bit lower than the usual Mildmay standard; it's not hard to question the form even as it stands, either, as only the first 2 seemed to run to their best on the day. **Native River** has upped his form a notch with cheekpieces on the last twice, now achieving the sort of ratings that looked likely after he won a Grade 2 at Newbury earlier in the season, dropping back in trip no problem here as Richard Johnson, who was riding him for the first time, made full use of his stamina with an excellent, positive ride that suited down to the ground; made all, jumped well in main, hit twelfth, driven soon after, tackled 3 out but found plenty and proved determined; he's a likeable type even though he has a lazy streak and he's stood up well to a busy schedule this season, Punchestown reportedly an option for him in another few weeks. **Henri Parry Morgan** is really thriving on racing, the fitting of a tongue strap seemingly having made a big difference as he's not looked back since it went on, backing up every bit and more of his recent impressive handicap wins in this much higher grade; prominent, travelled and jumped well, chased leader soon after 3 out, kept on; he's likely to stay long distances and appeals as a National type for the future. **Blaklion** ran creditably without quite matching the form of his RSA win last month, that big effort perhaps having taken the edge off slightly; chased leaders, ridden 4 out, close up 3 out, held between last 2, one paced. **Un Temps Pour Tout** set the clear standard after his authoritative display in a strong handicap at Cheltenham but must have been feeling the effects of that effort, when clearly primed for the day, as he was some way off repeating it and looked a tired horse in the end; prominent, went with enthusiasm, untidy fourth, every chance 3 out, weakened between last 2; although he doesn't always show it there's no doubt that he's a high-class horse on his day, over both hurdles and fences. **Ballyalton** didn't get home over the longest trip he's ever tackled but shaped as if still in good form until that told; in touch, not settle fully, effort approaching 3 out, weakened, found the test too much; he's best up to 2¾m. **Roi des Francs** disappointed in a first-time hood, producing a laboured effort; raced off the pace, off the bridle long way out, not fluent fifth, struggling when mistake fourteenth, never on terms; may benefit from a break. **Out Sam** hasn't done himself justice in more competitive races the last twice, possibly just having gone off the boil a little, although softer ground seems ideal (all wins on soft or heavy); held up, hit seventh, struggling when bad mistake fifteenth, soon done with, eased off; he's still one to keep the faith with for next season with some of the valuable handicap chases in mind. **Otago Trail** after 11 weeks off, can have a line put through this run; held up, all but came down eighth, pulled up quickly.

JLT Melling Chase (Grade 1) (1) 2m 3f 200y

Pos	Btn	Horse	Age	Wgt	Eq	Trainer	Jockey	SP
1		GOD'S OWN (IRE)	8	11-10		Tom George	Paddy Brennan	10/1
2	2¾	AL FEROF (FR)	11	11-10		Dan Skelton	Harry Skelton	15/2
3	9	CLARCAM (FR)	6	11-10	(t)	Gordon Elliott, Ireland	B. J. Cooper	28/1
4	22	SOMERSBY (IRE)	12	11-10	(s)	Mick Channon	Brian Hughes	28/1
5	5	VIBRATO VALTAT (FR)	7	11-10	(t)	Paul Nicholls	Sam Twiston-Davies	14/1
F		VAUTOUR (FR)	7	11-10		W. P. Mullins, Ireland	R. Walsh	1/5f

6 ran Race Time 5m 08.20 Closing Sectional (3.15f): 49.5s (98.5%) Winning Owner: Crossed Fingers Partnership

Vautour is an outstanding chaser and he dominated the ratings and market for this year's Melling but the race was thrown wide open, and obviously made much weaker, when he departed at the ninth fence; it was still a classy performance from God's Own to see off Al Ferof, although it's hardly form with great depth as neither Somersby nor Vibrato Valtat ran their race. **God's Own** had the door left ajar by Vautour's departure but still should be credited with improvement for beating Al Ferof, rated 6 lb his superior coming into the race, even if that rival wasn't quite at his very best, particularly as he dealt with him quite comfortably, soon putting a seal on the race once asked to do so; tracked pace fourth, loomed up 3 out, produced to lead soon after 2 out, in control when jumped right last, idled, kept up to work; he's been most reliable at the big spring meetings for the last 3 seasons now and ought to give another good account at Punchestown next. **Al Ferof** understandably hasn't raced too many times this season, connections no doubt wanting to keep him relatively fresh, and that's surely helping him to hold his form as he is, a little below his very best here but still running well; held up, took strong hold, went prominent eighth, left second next, led soon after 3 out, headed between last 2, rallied, pulled clear of remainder. **Clarcam** isn't quite up to this level but bounced back to his best after 12 weeks off, primed for the meeting unlike the rest of the field, and clearly it's a track that suits him well (won the Manifesto here last season); never far away, went with zest, left in front ninth, hit 3 out, headed soon after, one paced. **Somersby** ran one of his lesser races and was retired after the race, ending what has been a fine career that's included many cracking runs in the biggest races, including a Grade 1 success in the Clarence House at Ascot in 2012; in touch, lost place eighth, held 3 out, faded. **Vibrato Valtat** was let down by his jumping little more than 3 weeks after falling at Cheltenham, his confidence perhaps knocked by that; held up, made mistakes, lost touch after thirteenth. **Vautour** is a superb jumper 99% of the time but a rare blip cost him on this occasion, getting in too tight to the ninth, clipping the top and coming down, tanking along in front at the time, looking in a great rhythm up to that point and sure to have taken all the beating; he got up fine and galloped off straight away, so it ought not to have left too much of a mark.

AINTREE Saturday April 9
Race 3: GOOD to SOFT; Remainder: SOFT

Liverpool Stayers' Hurdle (Grade 1) (1) 3m 149y

Pos	Btn	Horse	Age	Wgt	Eq	Trainer	Jockey	SP
1		THISTLECRACK	8	11-7		Colin Tizzard	Tom Scudamore	2/7f
2	7	SHANESHILL (IRE)	7	11-7		W. P. Mullins, Ireland	P. Townend	8/1
3	5	PRINCE OF SCARS (IRE)	6	11-7		Gordon Elliott, Ireland	B. J. Cooper	10/1
4	2¾	SERIENSCHOCK (GER)	8	11-7	(t)	Mlle A. Rosa, France	Ludovic Philipperon	66/1
5	2	DIFFERENT GRAVEY (IRE)	6	11-7		Nicky Henderson	Nico de Boinville	5/1
6	19	AQALIM	6	11-7	(b)	John Ferguson	Aidan Coleman	50/1

6 ran Race Time 6m 33.60 Closing Sectional (3.10f): 44.40s (111.3%) Winning Owner: John and Heather Snook

Thistlecrack didn't face the depth of opposition as he had at Cheltenham, and nor did he have to run to the same level he'd shown there, but this was still a totally dominant performance, this division his for as long as he remains in this form, though a switch to chasing may yet be made next season; he ended up making his own running, at no great pace, but coped well with that, the sense that he's totally straightforward once again coming through. **Thistlecrack** made the most of a good opportunity, completing a 5-timer with loads to spare, clearly adaptable with regard to tactics, everything said about his performance in the World Hurdle still holding good; dictated, tanked along, jumped superbly, bar untidy 2 out, drew clear after, impressive. **Shaneshill** ran well back over hurdles, drafted in to help the stable's cause in the battle for the trainers' title, his stable short on options for long-distances hurdles, likely to be back over fences after this; held up, took keen hold, smooth headway straight, chased leader after 2 out, no impression on winner. **Prince of Scars** was below form after 3 months off, not so well served by the way this developed as he had been last time (when capitalising on World Hurdle runner-up Alpha des Obeaux's underperformance), his jumping not up to scratch, either; held up, not fluent from eighth, steady headway straight, never a threat. **Serienschock** with David Pipe last season, had won at listed level in France this winter and ran well upped in grade, the effort of trying to chase down the winner telling late on; in touch, travelled well, chased leader straight, shaken up 2 out, effort flattened out. **Different Gravey** upped markedly in trip and up in grade, plainly failed to stay and would have been better off against Annie Power earlier in the week (though his stable had another candidate in that, also a non-stayer in his chosen race); tracked pace, travelled well, ridden after 4 out, folded straight; he looked a top-class prospect at Ascot, though it may be as a novice chaser next season that he shows it. **Aqalim** faced a stiff task and was well held after 4 months off, his lack of enthusiasm not helping an already forlorn cause after halfway; held up, not fluent sixth, labouring circuit out, downed tools.

PUNCHESTOWN Wednesday April 27
GOOD to SOFT

Bibby Financial Services Ireland Punchestown Gold Cup Chase (Grade 1) 3m1f

Pos	Btn	Horse	Age	Wgt	Eq	Trainer	Jockey	SP
1		CARLINGFORD LOUGH (IRE)	10	11-10		John E. Kiely, Ireland	Barry Geraghty	12/1
2	4½	DJAKADAM (FR)	7	11-10		W. P. Mullins, Ireland	R. Walsh	9/2
3	2	DON POLI (IRE)	7	11-10		W. P. Mullins, Ireland	B. J. Cooper	6/1
4	nk	CUE CARD	10	11-10	(t)	Colin Tizzard	Paddy Brennan	4/6f
5	21	FOXROCK (IRE)	8	11-10	(b+t)	T. M. Walsh, Ireland	Denis O'Regan	33/1
F		ROAD TO RICHES (IRE)	9	11-10		Noel Meade, Ireland	Davy Russell	7/1

6 ran Race Time 6m 21.30 Closing Sectional (3.50f): 50.9s (104.9%) Winning Owner: Mr John P. McManus

The absence of both Don Cossack and Vautour may have taken a little shine off what is one of Ireland's most prestigious chases in the build-up, but it still looked a representative renewal, the field having accumulated 6 Grade 1 chase victories between them already this season, including the Betfair Chase, King George VI Chase, Lexus Chase and the Irish Gold Cup; However, with Road To Riches crashing out at the second last and the main protagonists clearly below their best, particularly the standard-setting Cue Card for whom this seemed one race too many, it's fair to assume that the contest didn't take as much winning as might have been expected, though it would be unjust to not to give credit where credit is due in relation to Carlingford Lough, who confirmed himself a top-class performer in landing his fifth Grade 1 success in this sphere. **Carlingford Lough** hasn't always received the credit he deserves, but is undoubtedly a top-class chaser when things fall right for him and proved better than ever in landing his second Grade 1 success of the season (fifth overall), once more seen to very good effect in playing his hand later than the trio that followed him home, reversing Gold Cup form with those particular rivals in the process; waited with, lost momentum when slow tenth, pushed along before 4 out, headway entering straight, close up 2 out, led last, forged clear run-in; a consistent sort overall, he's likely to be campaigned with the same races in mind next season. **Djakadam** shaped well for a long way, but again failed to match the level of performance he showed at Cheltenham, that effort understandably taking the edge off him the last twice; never far away, went prominent fifth, challenged from 3 out, left in front next, headed last, kept on, no impression on winner; a top-class chaser, he will remain a fixture at the top level in 2016/17. **Don Poli** ran just respectably, possibly just feeling the effects of a hard race at Aintree less than 3 weeks earlier; chased leaders, reminders after seventh, crept closer early final circuit, close up from 5 out, ridden approaching straight, one paced but rallied to regain third on run-in; headgear remains an option next season, but he looks sure to win more good races in 2016/17 regardless. **Cue Card** failed to meet expectations, possibly finding the race coming too soon after his Cheltenham and Aintree exertions, though this performance shouldn't detract from what has been an almost unbelievable revival over the past 6 months, 3 grade 1 victories marking him down as one the elite performers in the staying division at present and, though he'll be rising 11 in 2016/17, he will remain very difficult to beat in this sphere, particularly with the career of Don Cossack seemingly up in the air; soon steadied, took strong hold, crept closer before 5 out, ridden from 3 out, every chance between last 2, one paced. **Foxrock** back up in trip, predictably found this too competitive, his best efforts at this level having come in races with much less depth; prominent, not fluent fifth, lost place after 5 out, beaten soon after next. **Road To Riches** hasn't quite been able to reach the heights he did in 2014/15, but was in the process of running his best race for some time when departing in x-rated fashion late on, the fact he only suffered superficial cuts miraculous given the severe nature of his exit; led, travelled fluently, driven entering straight, still a length up and responding when fell heavily 2 out, looked sure to be involved.

PUNCHESTOWN Thursday April 28
GOOD to SOFT, Cross country course: GOOD to FIRM

Ladbrokes Champion Stayers Hurdle (Grade 1) 3m

Pos	Btn	Horse	Age	Wgt	Eq	Trainer	Jockey	SP
1		ONE TRACK MIND (IRE)	6	11-10		Warren Greatrex	G. Sheehan	10/1
2	2¼	JENNIES JEWEL (IRE)	9	11-3		Jarlath P. Fahey, Ireland	I. J. McCarthy	33/1
3	8	ALPHA DES OBEAUX (FR)	6	11-10		M. F. Morris, Ireland	B. J. Cooper	1/2f
4	1¾	DIAMOND KING (IRE)	8	11-10	(t)	Gordon Elliott, Ireland	Davy Russell	11/2
5	3¾	IF IN DOUBT (IRE)	8	11-10		Philip Hobbs	Barry Geraghty	10/1
6	13	LIEUTENANT COLONEL	7	11-10		Ms Sandra Hughes, Ireland	D. J. Mullins	16/1
7	21	THOUSAND STARS (FR)	12	11-10	(s)	W. P. Mullins, Ireland	P. Townend	25/1
8	18	LEGACY GOLD (IRE)	8	11-3		Stuart Crawford, Ireland	A. E. Lynch	28/1
F		SHANESHILL (IRE)	7	11-10		W. P. Mullins, Ireland	R. Walsh	7/2

9 ran   Race Time 6m 08.10   Closing Sectional (4.45f): 68.0s (100.4%)   Winning Owner: Mr Andy Weller

In the absence of Thistlecrack, the undisputed star of this division, this had a best of the rest feel about it, the runners-up in the equivalent contests at Cheltenham and Aintree taking on the winner of the Coral Cup, but as has been the case on a few occasions this week, it threw up a bit of a surprise result, One Track Mind the main beneficiary of Shaneshill's last-flight fall; the leaders pressed on some way out which meant it turned into a thorough test. **One Track Mind** freshened up after a good effort in the Rendlesham, took the step up in grade in his stride, deserving plenty of credit for that alone, all the while acknowledging that this may not have taken a great deal of winning, few giving their running and Shaneshill looking poised to pounce when crashing out at the last; close up, pushed along before 5 out, led under pressure after 2 out, tackled last, left clear there, kept going well; likely to be a big player in this division if kept hurdling next term, especially if Thistlecrack goes chasing, but connections are reportedly very keen to try him over fences, the RSA likely to be his main target. **Jennies Jewel** had reportedly been covered by Presenting since last seen, which may, at least in part, explain this seemingly much improved performance, doing very well to get as close as she did after taking a while to warm to her task in the jumping department; mid-division, early mistakes, headway before 3 out, close up entering straight, every chance last, kept on; a thoroughly likeable mare, this was reportedly her last race. **Alpha des Obeaux** turned in a rather flat display, possibly not quite over the exertions of chasing home Thistlecrack at Cheltenham, although hasn't really won the races one with his ability ought to have; chased leaders, pushed along before 2 out, one paced. **Diamond King** ran at least as well in defeat as when winning the time before, the 3f longer trip just appearing to stretch him; dropped out, loomed up 2 out, pushed along entering straight, effort flattened out; capable of winning lesser graded races over hurdles, though chasing surely beckons, already an 8-y-o after all. **If In Doubt** up in grade, found run of good form coming to a halt, not the first this week to find this a bridge too far having already taken in Cheltenham and Aintree; held up, blundered second, pushed along briefly early final circuit, driven 4 out, merely passed beaten horses. **Lieutenant Colonel** without a tongue strap this time, again ran below form in what has been a rather stop-start campaign; made running, not always fluent, ridden when flattened 2 out, headed soon after, no extra; open to improvement over fences, he is likely to be back in that sphere next time. **Thousand Stars** not the force of old, ran poorly after 6 months off, a few uncharacteristic jumping errors not helping his cause; held up, pecked third, pushed along before 4 out, bad mistake there, no further impression. **Legacy Gold** failed to stay this 3f longer trip, the way she went through the race suggesting she is still in good form; mid-division, ridden after 3 out, weakened early in straight. **Shaneshill** kept hurdling after a good effort at Aintree, can be considered an unlucky loser, less than a length down and seemingly going best when crashing out at the last; patiently ridden, smooth headway before home turn, hung right early in straight, yet to be asked for effort when fell heavily last; quickly made up into a smart novice chaser this term but will reportedly be kept to the smaller obstacles in the short term.

TIMEFORM'S BEST OF 2015/16

One hundred and eighty! It doesn't get any better in darts, and it's a huge rating for a jumper to score on the Timeform scale too, so for four chasers—Don Cossack, Cue Card, Vautour and the novice Douvan—to reach that level in 2015/16 was indicative of a vintage season. Douvan, potentially one of the best we've seen, is all about the future but it was names from the past that made many of the headlines, comebacks of one sort or another from injury or loss of form behind the success stories of Sprinter Sacre, Cue Card and My Tent Or Yours to name but three. There were some absentees too; neither Coneygree nor Faugheen were able to defend their respective Cheltenham titles in the Gold Cup and Champion Hurdle, while the void left by Tony McCoy's retirement was readily filled—after a sixteen-year wait—by Richard Johnson who had the jockeys' championship wrapped up by Christmas. The trainers' championship, on the other hand, see-sawed to a dramatic conclusion on the final day of the season when Paul Nicholls managed to hold off the challenge of Willie Mullins who went close to being champion on both sides of the Irish Sea. Dominant as he was, Mullins was only part of wider Irish success in Britain, with the stables of Gordon Elliott and Mouse Morris taking the Gold Cup and Grand National back to Ireland.

Staying Chasers

It was a pity that falls spoiled both clashes between the best chasers in Britain and Ireland. **Don Cossack** (c183) came down two out in the King George at Kempton won by **Cue Card** (c181), while it was the latter's turn to hit the deck three from home in the Gold Cup won by Don Cossack. For our money, the King George was the race of the season judged purely on quality, with another outstanding chaser **Vautour** (c180) going down by a head to Cue Card, though Don Cossack may well have beaten the pair of them had he stood up. The winner of ten of his last twelve starts, Don Cossack was injured after Cheltenham but there are hopes he'll be back to defend his Gold Cup title. The resurgence of Cue Card was one of the stories of the season when his wins also included a second Betfair Chase and a victory over the placed horses from the Gold Cup, **Don Poli** (c170) and **Djakadam** (c175), in the Bowl at Aintree. Vautour missed the Gold Cup (in which the same owners' Djakadam was runner-up for the second year)

Vautour leads Cue Card over the last in a thrilling King George

when controversially switched to the Ryanair instead to win at Cheltenham for the third year running. Irish domination of the Gold Cup was completed by fourth-placed **Carlingford Lough** (c167) who won the Irish Gold Cup for the second year (from **Road To Riches** (c168)) and then beat the below-par trio of Djakadam, Don Poli and Cue Card in the Punchestown Gold Cup. 2015 Gold Cup winner **Coneygree** (c171p) had just two rivals to beat on his return at Sandown before missing the rest of the season but could re-enter the Gold Cup picture this term, though **Silviniaco Conti** (c169), pulled up in the Grand National, has his work cut out to return to the top table, winning only a substandard Ascot Chase. The other top-class chasers who deserves a mention are the front-running grey **Smad Place** (c166), who won both the Hennessy Gold Cup and the Cotswold Chase, and **Many Clouds** (c166), who proved as good as ever when trying to give 5 lb to Don Poli at Aintree in December.

Two-Mile Chasers

The greatest comeback of the season surely belonged to **Sprinter Sacre** (c179) who regained the Queen Mother Champion Chase crown which he had won so outstandingly three years earlier. Pulled up in the 2015 renewal, Sprinter Sacre might not have been back to his brilliant best, but he was more than good enough at Cheltenham for odds-on favourite **Un de Sceaux** (c174) who was beaten for the first time in completed starts over fences. Sprinter Sacre won all four of his outings, including the Desert Orchid Chase at Kempton in a thrilling finish with another former Champion Chase winner **Sire de Grugy** (c167) and rounded off the season with a more emphatic beating of Un de Sceaux in the Celebration Chase at Sandown in which the latter's jumping let him down. Sire de Grugy won the Tingle Creek at Sandown, though only after surviving a stewards enquiry having collided in mid-air with **Special Tiara** (c169) jumping the last, the latter going on to finish third in the Champion Chase for the second year running. Runner-up to Un de Sceaux in the Clarence House Chase at Ascot in which his stable-companion **Traffic Fluide** (c162p) finished third on his only start of the season, Sire de Grugy finished well held subsequently behind Sprinter Sacre at both Cheltenham and Sandown. **God's Own** (c168) was a good fourth at Cheltenham but went on to do better still at the other big festivals, winning the Melling Chase at Aintree and then overturning odds-on Vautour, who'd fallen in the Melling, in the Champion Chase at Punchestown in which there was another significant comeback from Sprinter Sacre's stable-companion **Simonsig** (c164) in third on just his second start since winning the 2013 Arkle.

Novice Chasers

Head and shoulders above his fellow novices, **Douvan** (c180p)—memorably described by trainer Willie Mullins as 'a different species'—is the most exciting jumper in training, already up with the best established chasers on ratings and with the promise of better still to come. The only question about him is whether he'll remain at two miles or be stepped up in trip—either way he'll take all the beating in whichever races he turns up. His campaign took in five Grade 1 novices, jumping superbly on the way to winning the Arkle, even more impressive when beating the Arkle fourth **The Game Changer** (c157+) in the Maghull at Aintree and then completing a rare hat-trick at the big spring festivals in majestic fashion when beating The Game Changer again in the Ryanair Novices' at Punchestown. No other novices really stood out among the chasing pack, though, exceptionally, their ranks did include the now-retired Grand National winner **Rule The World** (c156) whose Aintree win turned out to be his only success as a chaser in what was his second season over fences! Other novices to win in open handicap company included **Un Temps Pour Tout** (c161), who put up the best effort by a British-trained novice when winning the Ultima Handicap Chase at Cheltenham, and the Scottish Grand National winner **Vicente** (c152) who had earlier finished fifth in the National Hunt Chase won by **Minella Rocco** (c153p). **Native River** (c152p) was runner-up in the four-miler but went one better in the Mildmay Novices' at Aintree where he had the RSA winner **Blaklion** (c150) and Un Temps Pour Tout behind him. Douvan's stablemates in the novice ranks included the JLT winner **Black**

Douvan (left) on his way to his seven-length romp in the Arkle

Hercules (c154p) who replaced the injured but promising **Killultagh Vic** (c154p) in that contest and **Avant Tout** (c155p) who won the novices' handicap at Punchestown under a big weight.

Staying Hurdlers

No division was dominated to quite the extent this one was by the Colin Tizzard-trained **Thistlecrack** (h174p). His five-timer in the Long Distance Hurdle at Newbury, the Long Walk at Ascot, the Cleeve followed by the World Hurdle at Cheltenham, and then the Liverpool Hurdle at Aintree was identical to that completed by Big Buck's in the 2011/12 season and he could hardly have done any more—or done it more easily, especially at Cheltenham—though a setback prevented him going to Punchestown. Such was the impression Thistlecrack made that he's favourite for the Gold Cup without having jumped a fence in public yet. The other staying hurdlers had to share what was left in the races Thistlecrack didn't contest. The Gigginstown pair **Prince of Scars** (h163) and **Alpha des Obeaux** (h162) finished first and second in Leopardstown's Christmas Hurdle before proving no match for Thistlecrack in Britain, Alpha des Obeaux runner-up in the World Hurdle and Prince of Scars third at Aintree. The Cleeve runner-up **Ptit Zig** (h162) had to go back to his native France to land a big prize in the Grande Course de Haies d'Auteuil for Paul Nicholls. **Cole Harden** (h156) was a well-beaten fourth in his bid to retain his World Hurdle crown but his trainer Warren Greatrex unearthed another high-class stayer in **One Track Mind** (h160) who profited from the fall of

Liverpool Hurdle runner-up **Shaneshill** (h158) to win the Champion Stayers' Hurdle at Punchestown. **Reve de Sivola**'s (h161) bid to win a fourth Long Walk Hurdle was foiled by Thistlecrack but he gained compensation of sorts by beating One Track Mind in the Rendlesham Hurdle at Haydock, while **Kilcooley** (h161) beat former Champion Hurdle winner **Rock On Ruby** (h160) (retired after winning the Ascot Hurdle next time) in the West Yorkshire Hurdle at Wetherby but was pulled up in the World Hurdle on his only subsequent start.

Two-Mile Hurdlers

Faugheen's (h176) season began with his first ever defeat and, worse still, ended prematurely with injury that prevented a successful defence of his Champion Hurdle title, something he was long odds-on to do. In between, though, he proved better than ever, easily winning a second Christmas Hurdle at Kempton (his defeat of the **The New One** (159x—the 'x' has gone on since falling at Aintree on his final outing) illustrating the continued weakness of the two-mile hurdle division in Britain) before a crushing fifteen-length victory over stable-companions **Arctic Fire** (h165) and **Nichols Canyon** (h164) in the Irish Champion Hurdle at Leopardstown. 2015 Champion Hurdle runner-up Arctic Fire also missed going back to Cheltenham, but Nichols Canyon, who'd inflicted that shock defeat on Faugheen in the Morgiana Hurdle at Punchestown in November, finished third in the Champion Hurdle. With Faugheen out, **Annie Power** (h170+) made a timely return from her own setback to deputise successfully for her stable-companion in the Champion Hurdle and then beat the placed horses again in even more emphatic fashion in the Aintree Hurdle. Illustrating the extraordinary strength in depth at their disposal, it was a third Mullins/Ricci hurdler who did duty in the Punchestown Champion Hurdle which was won by the David Nicholson Mares' Hurdle winner **Vroum Vroum Mag** (h155p) from the Henry de Bromhead-trained Fighting Fifth Hurdle winner **Identity Thief** (h157) who had finished only sixth at Cheltenham. Fighting Fifth runner-up **Top Notch** (h158) was one of five runners for Nicky Henderson in the Champion Hurdle, finishing fifth, but it was 2014 runner-up **My Tent Or Yours** (h164) who fared best of them to be second again, a remarkable feat given an absence of the best part of two years beforehand.

Novice Hurdlers

The highest-rated British-trained hurdler over two miles was, in fact, a novice, with the Nicky Henderson-trained **Altior** (h167p) going unbeaten in five starts. He was impressive in accounting for Willie Mullins' highly-touted **Min** (h153+) in the Supreme Novices' at Cheltenham, while the winner's stable-companion **Buveur d'Air** (h152p) finished third before going on to success in the Top Novices' at Aintree. Two more really good prospects—both unbeaten at the time—locked horns in the Neptune

Novices' at the Festival, with **Yorkhill** (h163p) and **Yanworth** (h158p) pulling clear of their rivals though not in the order the betting suggested. The Alan King-trained Yanworth wasn't seen out afterwards but Yorkhill, already successful in the Tolworth Novices' over two miles at Sandown, followed up at Aintree in the Mersey Novices' but was turned over by outsider **Don't Touch It** (h152) when it was a case of one race too many for him at Punchestown. Yorkhill's stable-companion **Petit Mouchoir** (h151), who looks a chaser in the making, also ran at all three major Festivals and went down only narrowly behind Buveur d'Air at Aintree and Don't Touch It at Punchestown. Having his third season over hurdles, but his first with Harry Fry, the much-improved **Unowhatimeanharry** (h147p) won all five of his races, the last of them the Albert Bartlett Novices' at Cheltenham to be the top staying novice. However, the younger pair **Ballyoptic** (h144p) and **Bellshill** (h146), who fought out the finish of the Sefton at Aintree, have more scope for progress (particularly over fences), Bellshill gaining compensation at Punchestown. The first two in the Triumph Hurdle stood out among the juvenile hurdlers, with the filly **Apple's Jade** (h157p) turning the tables on her Cheltenham conqueror **Ivanovich Gorbatov** (h156+) in no uncertain terms under much softer conditions at Aintree and then beating him again at Punchestown.

Altior fights off Min to win the Supreme Novices' Hurdle

2015/16 STATISTICS

TRAINERS (1,2,3 earnings)		Horses	Indiv'l Wnrs	Races Won	Runs	% Strike Rate	Stakes £
1	W. P. Mullins, Ireland	88	20	27	159	17.0	2,271,652
2	Paul Nicholls	162	83	122	568	21.5	2,248,607
3	Nicky Henderson	152	57	81	414	19.6	1,529,272
4	Colin Tizzard	58	27	50	323	15.5	1,405,640
5	Philip Hobbs	144	72	113	523	21.6	1,298,246
6	Dan Skelton	148	73	104	529	19.7	1,150,854
7	Nigel Twiston-Davies	110	45	72	482	14.9	1,113,032
8	David Pipe	126	50	80	571	14.0	1,066,025
9	Alan King	123	43	68	403	16.9	969,590
10	Venetia Williams	100	38	56	419	13.4	926,751

JOCKEYS (by winners)		1st	2nd	3rd	Unpl	Total Rides	% Strike Rate
1	Richard Johnson	235	186	155	468	1044	22.5
2	Aidan Coleman	129	112	103	397	741	17.5
3	Sam Twiston-Davies	128	118	89	406	741	17.3
4	Noel Fehily	122	106	85	350	663	18.4
5	Brian Hughes	103	131	113	388	735	14.0
6	Harry Skelton	101	79	57	215	452	22.3
7	Tom Scudamore	85	70	67	315	537	15.8
8	Paddy Brennan	75	70	55	263	463	16.2
9	Gavin Sheehan	72	64	51	253	440	16.4
10	Nico de Boinville	69	34	34	190	327	21.1

SIRES OF WINNERS (1,2,3 earnings)		Races Won	Runs	% Strike Rate	Stakes £
1	King's Theatre (by Sadler's Wells)	123	806	15.3	1,939,009
2	Kayf Tara (by Sadler's Wells)	145	946	15.3	1,830,884
3	Flemensfirth (by Alleged)	115	701	16.4	1,220,035
4	Presenting (by Mtoto)	109	812	13.4	1,126,012
5	Milan (by Sadler's Wells)	99	770	12.9	913,499
6	Beneficial (by Top Ville)	81	711	11.4	897,560
7	Westerner (by Danehill)	72	473	15.2	788,394
8	Midnight Legend (by Night Shift)	68	617	11.0	737,011
9	Oscar (by Sadler's Wells)	78	571	13.7	670,058
10	Sulamani (by Hernando)	12	88	13.6	649,155

LEADING HORSES (1,2,3 earnings)		Races Won	Runs	Stakes £
1	Rule The World 9 b.g Sulamani–Elaine Tully	1	1	561,300
2	Thistlecrack 8 b.g Kayf Tara–Ardstown	5	5	372,003
3	Cue Card 10 b.g King's Theatre–Wicked Crack	4	5	368,581
4	Annie Power 8 ch.m Shirocco–Anno Luce	2	2	361,374
5	Sprinter Sacre 10 b/br.g Network–Fatima III	4	4	358,786
6	Don Cossack 9 br.g Sholokhov–Depeche Toi	1	2	327,463
7	The Last Samuri 8 ch.g Flemensfirth–Howaboutthis	2	4	278,048
8	Vautour 7 b.g Robin des Champs–Gazelle de Mai	2	4	262,148
9	Smad Place 9 gr.g Smadoun–Bienna Star	3	5	184,114
10	Un de Sceaux 8 b.g Denham Red–Hotesse de Sceaux	1	3	172,696

SECTION

THE TIMEFORM TOP 100

Hurdlers

176	Faugheen
174p	Thistlecrack
170+	Annie Power (f)
167p	Altior
166+	Un de Sceaux
165	Arctic Fire
164	My Tent Or Yours
164	Nichols Canyon
163p	Yorkhill
163	Prince of Scars
162	Alpha des Obeaux
162	Ptit Zig
161	Kilcooley
161	Reve de Sivola
160	One Track Mind
160	Rock On Ruby
159x	The New One
158p	Yanworth
158	Shaneshill
158	Top Notch
157p	Apple's Jade (f)
157	Identity Thief
156+	Ivanovich Gorbatov
156	Camping Ground
156	Cole Harden
156	Diakali
156	Different Gravey
156	Hargam
156	Silsol
156	Wicklow Brave
155p	Vroum Vroum Mag (f)
155	Court Minstrel
155	Diamond King
155	Irving
155	Lil Rockerfeller
155	Taglietelle
154	Martello Tower
154	Old Guard
153+	Min
153	Bobs Worth
153	Sempre Medici

153	Thousand Stars
152p	Buveur d'Air
152	Don't Touch It
152	Ivan Grozny
152	Thomas Edison
151	Aubusson
151	Commissioned
151	If In Doubt
151	Jennies Jewel (f)
151	Petit Mouchoir
151	Simonsig
150	Charbel
149	Arbre de Vie
149	Cheltenian
149	Deputy Dan
149	Grumeti
149	Sign of A Victory
149	Ubak
149	Vaniteux
148	Arpege d'Alene
148	Brother Tedd
148	Dedigout
148	Lieutenant Colonel
148	Renneti
148	Sea Lord
148	Serienschock
148	Silviniaco Conti
147p	Unowhatimeanharry
147	Baradari
147	Broadway Buffalo
147	Champion Court
147	Fethard Player
147	Footpad
147	Gwencily Berbas
147	Monksland
147	Rock The Kasbah
147	Volnay de Thaix
147§	Aqalim
146	Al Ferof
146	Bellshill
146	Brain Power
146	Its'afreebee
146	Missed Approach

145p	Anibale Fly
145	Aristo du Plessis
145	Ballynagour
145	Bleu Et Rouge
145	Ibis du Rheu
145	Ittirad
145	Jolly's Cracked It
145	Might Bite
145	O O Seven
145	Rawnaq
145	Superb Story
145	Ted Veale
145	Tombstone
145	Value At Risk
145	War Sound
145x	At Fishers Cross

Chasers

183	Don Cossack
181	Cue Card
180p	Douvan
180	Vautour
179	Sprinter Sacre
175	Djakadam
174	Un de Sceaux
171p	Coneygree
170	Don Poli
169	Silviniaco Conti
169	Special Tiara
168	Al Ferof
168	God's Own
168	Road To Riches
168x	Menorah
167	Carlingford Lough
167	Sire de Grugy
167	Valseur Lido
166	Many Clouds
166	Smad Place
165	Irish Cavalier
164	Ptit Zig
164	Simonsig
163	Gilgamboa

162p	Traffic Fluide
162	O'Faolains Boy
161	Ballynagour
161	Sausalito Sunrise
161	Smashing
161	Un Temps Pour Tout
160	Dynaste
160	Felix Yonger
160	Flemenstar
160	Sound Investment
160	Top Gamble
160§	Wishfull Thinking
159	First Lieutenant
159	Holywell
159	Taquin du Seuil
159	Virak
158	Foxrock
158	Sam Winner
158	The Last Samuri
157+	Ar Mad
157+	Dodging Bullets
157+	No More Heroes
157	Simply Ned
157	Somersby
157	The Game Changer
157	Vaniteux
157	Vibrato Valtat
157x	Hidden Cyclone
157§	Third Intention
156p	Kylemore Lough
156	Arzal
156	Camping Ground
156	Clarcam
156	Rule The World
156	Saphir du Rheu
156§	On His Own
155p	Avant Tout
155	Boondooma
155	Houblon des Obeaux
155	Mala Beach
155	Triolo d'Alene
155	Village Vic
155	Wonderful Charm

155§	Twinlight
154p	Black Hercules
154p	Gallant Oscar
154p	Killultagh Vic
154p	Zabana
154	Claret Cloak
154	Rock The World
154	Sizing John
154x	Josses Hill
154§	Bright New Dawn
153p	Minella Rocco
153	Annacotty
153	Days Hotel
153	Outlander
153	Roi du Mee
153	Savello
153	Seeyouatmidnight
153	The Druids Nephew
153	Wounded Warrior
153x	Champagne West
153§	Rocky Creek
152p	Native River
152	Arthur's Oak
152	Blood Cotil
152	Cause of Causes
152	Grey Gold
152	Just A Par
152	Just Cameron
152	Royal Regatta
152	Tango de Juilley
152	The Young Master
152	Vicente
152	Wakanda
152§	Sadler's Risk

Juvenile Hurdlers

157p	Apple's Jade (f)
156+	Ivanovich Gorbatov
147	Footpad
145p	Adrien du Pont
144	Leoncavallo
143p	Allblak des Places
143p	Campeador
142p	Voix du Reve
141p	Clan des Obeaux
141?	Chic Name

140p	Koshari
140	Zubayr
139	Fixe Le Kap
139	Missy Tata (f)
138p	Let's Dance (f)
138	Gibralfaro
138	Romain de Senam
137	Jer's Girl (f)
137	Slowmotion (f)
136p	Tommy Silver
136	Connetable
136	Rashaan
136	Wolf of Windlesham
135	Diego du Charmil
135	Frodon
135	Sceau Royal
135	Who Dares Wins
133	Azzuri
133	Coo Star Sivola
133	Protek des Flos

Novice Hurdlers

167p	Altior
163p	Yorkhill
158p	Yanworth
153+	Min
152p	Buveur d'Air
152	Don't Touch It
151	Petit Mouchoir
150	Charbel
147p	Unowhatimeanharry
146	Bellshill
146	Brain Power
146	Its'afreebee
145p	Anibale Fly
145	Bleu Et Rouge
145	O O Seven
145	Tombstone
144p	Ballyoptic
144p	Emerging Force
144	Agrapart
144	Fagan
144	Le Prezien
144	Long Dog
143	Barters Hill
143	Bello Conti

143	Flying Angel
143	Gala Ball
143	Mister Miyagi
143	Shantou Village
143	Supasundae
142	North Hill Harvey

Novice Chasers

180p	Douvan
161	Un Temps Pour Tout
157+	Ar Mad
157+	No More Heroes
157	The Game Changer
157	Vaniteux
156p	Kylemore Lough
156	Arzal
156	Rule The World
155p	Avant Tout
154p	Black Hercules
154p	Killultagh Vic
154p	Zabana
154	Rock The World
154	Sizing John
153p	Minella Rocco
153	Outlander
153	Seeyouatmidnight
152p	Native River
152	Vicente
151+	Alisier d'Irlande
150p	Shaneshill
150p	Vivaldi Collonges
150+	More of That
150	Blaklion
150	Bristol de Mai
150	Monksland
149p	Henri Parry Morgan
149	Viconte du Noyer
148	L'Ami Serge

NH Flat Horses

123	Ballyandy
123	Blow By Blow
122+	Moon Racer
121	Bacardys
120	Battleford

120	Jenkins
119p	Betameche
118	High Bridge
118	Prince d'Aubrelle
118	The Minch
116p	Castello Sforza
116p	Invitation Only
116	Very Much So
115p	Westend Story
115	Coeur Blimey
115	Criq Rock
114p	Brahms de Clermont
114p	Lucky Pass
114	Augusta Kate (f)
114	Capitaine
114	Kayf Grace (f)
113	Rather Be
113	Willoughby Court
112	First Figaro
111p	Mr Big Shot
111	Bags Groove
111	La Bague Au Roi (f)
111	Our Dancing Dandy
110	Avenir d'Une Vie
110	Death Duty
110	New To This Town
110	Savoy Court

Hunter Chasers

138	On The Fringe
137	Marito
136	Pacha du Polder
135	Paint The Clouds
134	Current Event
133	Mendip Express
132	Moroman
128	On The Bridge
128	Salsify
128§	Major Malarkey
127	Dineur
127	Palypso de Creek
127	Pearlysteps
126	Twirling Magnet
125p	It Came To Pass

* Indicates best performance achieved in a race other than a hunter chase

PROMISING HORSES

A p symbol is used by Timeform to denote horses we believe are capable of improvement, with a P symbol suggesting a horse is capable of much better form. Below is a list of selected British-trained horses (plus those trained by Willie Mullins) with a p or P, listed under their current trainers.

KIM BAILEY

Aliandy (IRE) 5 b.g. h106p b91
Bonne Fee 9 b.m. c106p
Derrintogher Bliss (IRE) 7 b.g. c126p
Gold Man (IRE) 7 ch.g. ....h86p c–p
Kalanisi Glen (IRE) 6 br.g. h92p
Silver Kayf 4 gr.g. b93p

PETER BOWEN

Henri Parry Morgan 8 b.g. h123 c149p
Minella Daddy (IRE) 6 b.g. h127p

MARK BRADSTOCK

Coneygree 9 b.g. c171p

REBECCA CURTIS

Carningli (IRE) 7 b.g. c121p

GORDON ELLIOTT, IRELAND

Campeador (FR) 4 gr.g. h143p
De Plotting Shed (IRE) 6 b.g. ......h128p b110+
Fascino Rustico 8 b.g. c131p
Flaxen Flare (IRE) 7 ch.g. c124p
Free Expression (IRE) 7 b.g. c139p c145p
Sutton Place (IRE) 5 b.g. h141p
Western Home (IRE) 6 br.m. c120p

HARRY FRY

Activial (FR) 6 gr.g. h152 c144p
American (FR) 6 b.g. h128p
Behind Time (IRE) 5 b.g. h110p
Bitofapuzzle 8 b.m. c137p
Black Mischief 4 b.g. b97p
Meme's Horse (IRE) 6 b.g. h122p
Nitrogen (IRE) 9 b.g. c117p
Secret Door (IRE) 5 b.m. h111p
Space Oddity (FR) 5 b. or br.g. h116p
Unowhatimeanharry 8 b.g. h147p
Wotzizname (IRE) 6 b.g. h138p

TOM GEORGE

Battle of Shiloh (IRE) 7 b.g. h126p
Beni Light (FR) 5 b.g. b88p
Frosty Steel (IRE) 6 b.g. h100p c98p
Kk Lexion (IRE) 5 b.g. h108p

WARREN GREATREX

Aloomomo (FR) 6 b.g. c138p
At The Doubble (IRE) 7 b.g. h137p
Caitys Joy (GER) 6 b.m. h117p
Ilovemints 4 b.f. b105p
Out Sam 7 b.g. h141 c141p
Penn Lane (IRE) 5 b.g. h118p b104

MRS J. HARRINGTON, IRELAND

Forge Meadow (IRE) 4 b.f. b104p
Our Duke (IRE) 6 b.g. ....h133p b114+

NICKY HENDERSON

Altior (IRE) 6 b.g. h167p b115
Argante (FR) 7 b. or br.g. h120p
Baden (FR) 5 gr.g. h131p
Buveur d'Air (FR) 5 b.g. h152p
Clean Sheet (FR) 7 b.g. h131p
Consul de Thaix (FR) 4 b.g. h136p
Hurricane Higgins (IRE) 8 br.g. h136p
No Heretic 8 b.g. h117p
Polly's Pursuit (IRE) 4 b. or b.f. b83p
Pougne Bobbi (FR) 5 b. or br.g. h127p b97p
River Wylde (IRE) 5 b.g. b106p

PHILIP HOBBS

Bacchanel (FR) 5 b.g. h94p b91
Beau du Brizais (FR) 4 gr.g. b78p h97p
Bradford Bridge (IRE) 4 b.g. b77p
Captain Bocelli (IRE) 7 b.g. h105p b95
Casper King (IRE) 5 b.g. h124p
Lisheen Prince (IRE) 5 b.g. b85p
Longtown (IRE) 5 b.g. b81p
No Comment 5 br.g. ....h123p b106+
One Cool Scorpion (IRE) 5 b.g. h105p b95
Perform (IRE) 7 b.g. h138p
Poppy Kay 6 b.m. b100p
Roll The Dough (IRE) 7 b.g. h127p
Steal My Thunder (IRE) 5 gr.g. b82p
Three Faces West (IRE) 8 b.g. h130 c135p
Verni (FR) 7 ch.g. h121p
Wait For Me (FR) 6 b.g. h136p
Wishfull Dreaming (IRE) 8 b.g. ...b105+ h121p

MALCOLM JEFFERSON

Cloudy Dream (IRE) 6 gr.g. ....h141p b108+
Cyrus Darius 7 b.g. c140p
Gully's Edge 6 b.g. h132p b99
Mount Mews (IRE) 5 b.g. b113p

ALAN KING

Bastien (FR) 5 b.g. b87p
Chosen Well (IRE) 7 b.g. ....h127+ c117p
Duke of Sonning 4 ch.g. h124p
Herewego Herewego (IRE) 5 b.g. h118p
Informationisking (IRE) 5 b.g. b104p
Karezak (IRE) 5 b.g. h143 c111P
Laser Light (IRE) 5 b.g. b103p
Mia's Storm (IRE) 6 b.m. h118p b106
The Unit (IRE) 5 b.g. h113p b102

WINTER ESCAPE

Winter Escape (IRE) 5 b.g. h142P
Yanworth 6 ch.g. h158p
Zipple Back (IRE) 4 b.g. b91p

EMMA LAVELLE

Andy Kelly (IRE) 7 ch.g. c133p
Casino Markets (IRE) 8 br.g. ....h115p c131+
Fortunate George (IRE) 6 b.g. h123p
Hard As A Rock (FR) 5 b.g. b80p

KERRY LEE

Kris Spin (IRE) 5 b.g. ....h143 c–P
Kylemore Lough 7 b.g. c156p
Lady Beaufort 5 ch.m. b91p
Matchaway (IRE) 7 b.g. h119p
Sir Will (IRE) 5 b.g. h114p b101

CHARLIE LONGSDON

Our Kaempfer (IRE) 7 b.g. h143p
Quieto Sol (FR) 5 ch.g. h111p
Snow Leopardess 4 gr.f. b95p

A. J. MARTIN, IRELAND

Anibale Fly (FR) 6 b.g. h145p
Gallant Oscar (FR) 10 b.g. h129 c155p
Mydor (FR) 6 ch.g. h132 c117p
Noble Emperor (IRE) 8 b.g. ....h142p c142+

NOEL MEADE, IRELAND

De Name Escapes Me (IRE) 6 ch.g. h133p
Disko (FR) 5 gr.g. h126p b115p
Killer Miller (IRE) 7 b.g. h121p c135p

GARY MOORE

Draco's Code 5 b.g. h114p
Graasten (GER) 4 ch.g. h117p
Krugermac (IRE) 5 b. or br.g. h132p
Master of Speed (IRE) 4 ch.g. h115p
Remind Me Later (IRE) 7 b.g. h118p c122p
Stonegate 6 b.g. h91p
Traffic Fluide (FR) 6 b.g. c162p

NEIL MULHOLLAND

Admiral Kid (IRE) 5 b.g. b96p
Attractive Liason (IRE) 4 b.g. ....h–p
Carole's Vigilante (IRE) 5 ch.g. b92p
Champagne George (IRE) 6 gr.g. ...h113p b95
Halo Moon 8 br.g. c127p
Indian Brave (IRE) 5 b.g. h105p b84
Peter The Mayo Man (IRE) 6 ch.g. h121p
Sleep Easy 4 b.g. h135p
Solomn Grundy (IRE) 6 b.g. h115p
Soupy Soups (IRE) 5 ch.g. ....h107p b87+

W. P. MULLINS, IRELAND

Allblak des Places (FR) 4 b. or br.g........h145p
Apple's Jade (FR) 4 b.f........h157p
Arbre de Vie (FR) 6 b.g........h149 c140p
Avant Tout (FR) 6 ch.g........h145 c156p
Black Hercules (IRE) 7 b.g........c154p
Blazer (FR) 5 ch.g........h140 c110p
Bleu Berry (FR) 5 b.g........h118p
Burgas (FR) 5 b. or br.g........h132 c104p
Castello Sforza (IRE) 5 b.g........b117p
Daneking 7 b.g........h138 c127p
Invitation Only (IRE) 5 b.g........h116p
Killultagh Vic (IRE) 7 b.g........c154p
Koshari (FR) 4 br.g........h140p
Let's Dance (FR) 4 b.f........h138p
Listen Dear (IRE) 6 b.m........h134p c139p
Lucky Pass (FR) 5 ch.g........b114p
Pylonthepressure (IRE) 6 b.g........h125p b117
Ria d'Etel (FR) 4 b.f........h131p
Rolly Baby (FR) 11 b.g........h139p
Shaneshill (IRE) 7 b.g........h158 c150p
Tell Us More (IRE) 7 b.g........c142p
Valyssa Monterg (FR) 7 b. or br.m..h131 c125p
Village Mystic (FR) 5 b. or br.g........b109p
Voix du Reve (FR) 4 br.g........h142p
Vroum Vroum Mag (FR) 7 b.m....h155p c151P
Yorkhill (IRE) 6 ch.g........h163p b125p

PAUL NICHOLLS

Adrien du Pont (FR) 4 b.g........h145p
Alibi de Sivola (FR) 6 b. or br.g........h131p
Anatol (FR) 6 b.g........h136p c131p
Bill And Barn (IRE) 5 br.g........b83p
Brave Jaq (FR) 5 ch.g........h111p
Bugsie Malone (IRE) 6 b.g........h115p
Clan des Obeaux (FR) 4 b.g........h143p
Coup de Pinceau (FR) 4 b.g........b99p
El Bandit (IRE) 5 b. or br.g........h130p
Frodon (FR) 4 b.g........h135 c135p
Some Buckle (FR) 7 b.g........h134 c139p
Tommy Silver (FR) 4 b.g........h138p
Touch Kick (IRE) 5 b.g........b99p
Vivaldi Collonges (FR) 7 b.g........c150p
Whispering Storm (GER) 6 b.g........h115p
Winningtry (IRE) 5 b.g........b93p

FERGAL O'BRIEN

Mystifiable 8 gr.g........h111 c135p
War On The Rocks (IRE) 7 b.g........h107p b95

JONJO O'NEILL

Above Board (IRE) 5 b.g........b98p
Another Hero (IRE) 7 b.g........c135p
Beg To Differ (IRE) 6 ch.g........c143p
Benzel (IRE) 8 b.g........h109p
Call To Order 6 b.g........h108p b103
Celtic Tune (FR) 5 b.g........h96p
Dream Berry (FR) 5 gr.g........h122p
For Instance (IRE) 6 b.g........h114p b104
Go Conquer (IRE) 7 b.g........c135p
In The Rough (IRE) 7 b.g........c138p
It Is What It Is (IRE) 9 b.g........h–p c103p
Join The Clan (IRE) 7 b.g........h135 c128p
Lockstockandbarrel (IRE) 7 b.g........h133p c135p
Minella Rocco (IRE) 6 b.g........c153p

Powerful Symbol (IRE) 6 b.g........h106p b92
Suit Yourself (IRE) 7 b.g........h121p
Tried And Tested (IRE) 5 b.g........h116P
Which One Is Which 5 b.m........b98p

BEN PAULING

Always Lion (IRE) 6 b.g........h126p
Born To Succeed (IRE) 6 b.g........c101p
Kalanisi Circle (IRE) 4 b.g........b89p
Smoking Dixie (IRE) 5 ch.g........b80p

DAVID PIPE

Bird d'Estruval (FR) 5 ch.g........h108p
Carqalin (FR) 4 gr.g........h96p
Eamon An Cnoic (IRE) 5 b.g........h103p b84
It'll Be Grand 7 b.g........h102p
Moon Racer (IRE) 7 b.g........b122+ h125P
Mr Big Shot (IRE) 5 br.g........b114p
Navanman (IRE) 7 b.g........h116p
The Minkle (IRE) 5 ch.g........h65p
Unique de Cotte (FR) 8 b.g........h138 c146p

NICKY RICHARDS

Ballyboker Breeze (IRE) 8 b.g........c132p
Conquer Gold (IRE) 6 b.m........h102p b88+
Hester Flemen (IRE) 8 ch.m........h134p c134p
Strait of Magellan (IRE) 4 ch.g........h–p

LUCINDA RUSSELL

Big River (IRE) 6 b.g........h117p
Chaz Michaels (IRE) 6 ch.g........h98p
Fifteen Kings (IRE) 6 b.g........h84p
Superior Command (IRE) 7 b.g........h95 c115p

OLIVER SHERWOOD

Coco Shambhala 8 b.m........h96p
Icing On The Cake (IRE) 6 b.g........h112p
Kings Bandit (IRE) 8 b.g........h142p c–p
Legend Lady 5 b.m........h113p
Mankala (IRE) 6 b.g........b80p
The Organist (IRE) 5 b.m........h135p b89p

DAN SKELTON

Abricot de L'Oasis (FR) 6 b.g........h127 c118p
Applesandpierres (IRE) 8 b.g........h113p
Asum 5 b.g........b89p
Beautiful Gem (FR) 6 ch.m........h92p
Bekkensfirth 7 b.g........h108 c134p
Betameche (FR) 5 gr.g........b119p
Bilzic (FR) 5 b. or br.g........h94p b94
Born Survivor (IRE) 5 b.g........h134p
Ch'tibello (FR) 5 b.g........h142p
Chap 6 ch.g........h–p b97
Djarkalin (FR) 4 b.g........b82p
Dragon de La Tour (FR) 5 b.g........h86p
Kasakh Noir (FR) 4 ch.g........h132p
Late Night Lily 5 b.m........h112p b95+
Meet The Legend 5 b.g........h142p b113
Micks Lad (IRE) 6 b.g........h101p
Mister Kalanisi (IRE) 7 b.g........h106p b84p
Mont Lachaux (FR) 3 b.c........h135p
Oldgrangewood 5 b.g........h118p
Pain Au Chocolat (FR) 5 b.g........h134 c143p
Red Tornado (FR) 4 ch.g........h134p
Robin Roe (IRE) 5 b.g........b98p

Stage One (IRE) 5 b.g........h120p
Two Taffs (IRE) 6 b.g........h135p

COLIN TIZZARD

Bramble Brook 6 b.g........h99p
Cucklington 5 b.g........h99 b90p
Native River (IRE) 6 ch.g........c152p
Thistlecrack 8 b.g........h174p

NIGEL TWISTON-DAVIES

Ballyarthur (IRE) 6 b.g........h113p
Ballyoptic (IRE) 6 b.g........h146p b67
Flying Angel (IRE) 5 gr.g........h143 c143p
Wholestone (IRE) 5 br.g........h117p b108p

TIM VAUGHAN

Satellite (IRE) 5 b.g........h124p
Theligny (FR) 5 gr.g........h118p

HARRY WHITTINGTON

Emerging Force (IRE) 6 b.g........h144p
Pink Play (IRE) 5 b.m........h120p b91p
Tolethorpe 5 ch.g........b106p

EVAN WILLIAMS

Aqua Dude (IRE) 6 br.g........h142p
Dark Spirit (IRE) 8 b.m........h135 c105p
Go Long (IRE) 6 b.g........h135p
In The Hold (IRE) 6 b.g........h96p
King's Odyssey (IRE) 7 b.g........c147p
Mac Gregory 5 b.g........h104p b91
On The Road (IRE) 6 b.g........h86p
Shrewd Tactics (IRE) 5 ch.g........b89p

NICK WILLIAMS

Aubusson (FR) 7 b.g........h151 c130p
Barranco Valley 5 b.g........h124p
Flying Tiger (IRE) 3 b.g........h121p
Tea For Two 7 b.g........h136 c146p

VENETIA WILLIAMS

Belami des Pictons (FR) 5 b.g........h127p
Bennys King (IRE) 5 b.g........h118p
Fionn Mac Cul (IRE) 5 b.g........h122p
Opera Rock (FR) 5 b.g........b87p

TRAINERS FOR COURSES

The following statistics show the most successful trainers over the past five seasons at each of the courses that stage National Hunt racing in England, Scotland and Wales. Impact Value is expressed as a factor of a trainer's number of winners compared to those expected to occur by chance. Market Value is expressed as the factor by which the % chance of an Industry Starting Price exceeds random, as implied by field size. For example, a horse that is shorter than 3/1 in a 4-runner field will have a Market Value above 1.

AINTREE

Trainer	Wins	Runs	Strike Rate	% Rivals Beaten	P/L	Run To Form %	Impact Value	Market Value
Nicky Henderson	35	178	19.66%	56.87	38.36	25.63	2.13	1.71
Paul Nicholls	18	170	10.59%	55.10	-37.45	16.02	1.18	1.69
Nigel Twiston-Davies	14	102	13.73%	57.37	0.82	27.07	1.53	1.43
Philip Hobbs	13	105	12.38%	57.71	-14.92	20.27	1.48	1.50
Peter Bowen	13	113	11.50%	50.90	-33.05	21.45	1.13	1.23
W. P. Mullins, Ireland	10	68	14.71%	60.73	-20.15	30.88	1.86	1.97
Jonjo O'Neill	10	96	10.42%	51.45	-42.95	18.91	1.19	1.49
Donald McCain	10	153	6.54%	44.97	-105.92	13.41	0.69	1.24
Alan King	10	84	11.90%	54.62	-5.75	27.80	1.23	1.57
Rebecca Curtis	8	51	15.69%	53.25	-20.26	19.61	1.55	1.39

ASCOT

Trainer	Wins	Runs	Strike Rate	% Rivals Beaten	P/L	Run To Form %	Impact Value	Market Value
Nicky Henderson	33	152	21.71%	60.11	-47.25	34.44	1.76	2.15
Paul Nicholls	32	149	21.48%	62.25	-16.09	41.19	1.64	1.57
Philip Hobbs	16	101	15.84%	63.86	-19.39	31.77	1.39	1.44
Alan King	16	94	17.02%	63.09	36.39	32.98	1.51	1.36
David Pipe	13	86	15.12%	55.53	-13.76	23.43	1.55	1.47
Venetia Williams	13	89	14.61%	54.82	28.5	27.26	1.31	1.21
Harry Fry	10	30	33.33%	70.27	12.84	51.96	3.00	1.78
Colin Tizzard	8	50	16.00%	51.98	2.21	30.00	1.27	1.06
Oliver Sherwood	6	29	20.69%	60.22	-4.68	53.10	1.77	1.32
Charlie Longsdon	6	66	9.09%	46.78	-2.5	18.76	0.81	1.24

AYR

Trainer	Wins	Runs	Strike Rate	% Rivals Beaten	P/L	Run To Form %	Impact Value	Market Value
Lucinda Russell	38	276	13.77%	54.31	-110.35	27.86	0.98	1.18
Nicky Richards	28	120	23.33%	56.83	-7.22	33.83	1.72	1.72
Donald McCain	26	116	22.41%	53.05	-27.21	28.33	1.51	1.85
Jim Goldie	19	162	11.73%	50.39	-35.46	24.04	0.91	1.10
N. W. Alexander	18	154	11.69%	48.45	-34.23	25.01	0.91	0.95
Stuart Crawford, Ireland	14	108	12.96%	55.39	-33.13	26.19	0.98	1.22
Paul Nicholls	12	38	31.58%	62.19	37.83	47.37	2.73	1.68
James Ewart	12	96	12.50%	50.80	-25.78	24.72	0.98	1.00
Martin Todhunter	8	58	13.79%	48.32	-9.03	28.30	1.03	1.04
J. J. Lambe, Ireland	7	42	16.67%	48.96	11.25	23.81	1.24	0.87

BANGOR-ON-DEE

Trainer	Wins	Runs	Strike Rate	% Rivals Beaten	P/L	Run To Form %	Impact Value	Market Value
Donald McCain	67	323	20.74%	56.10	-0.2	29.77	1.38	1.51
Rebecca Curtis	24	85	28.24%	62.51	2.53	41.45	1.88	1.74
Jonjo O'Neill	20	150	13.33%	53.11	-54.75	23.88	1.01	1.48
Charlie Longsdon	17	78	21.79%	56.20	-17.11	28.94	1.55	1.58
Venetia Williams	16	102	15.69%	53.23	-12.68	24.99	1.16	1.14
Nicky Henderson	14	51	27.45%	60.78	-12.53	39.97	1.98	2.57
Warren Greatrex	13	34	38.24%	67.18	30.59	44.29	3.03	2.00
Alan King	10	56	17.86%	56.82	-6.13	25.59	1.48	1.51
Nigel Twiston-Davies	9	57	15.79%	61.93	-3.5	38.18	1.27	1.53
Tim Vaughan	9	59	15.25%	52.10	4.38	24.15	1.02	1.28

CARLISLE

Trainer	Wins	Runs	Strike Rate	% Rivals Beaten	P/L	Run To Form %	Impact Value	Market Value
Donald McCain	36	201	17.91%	58.86	-66.82	28.71	1.30	1.76
Sue Smith	20	126	15.87%	51.94	-11.04	29.28	1.24	1.23
Nicky Richards	20	75	26.67%	60.17	34.14	35.26	2.10	1.61
Lucinda Russell	19	200	9.50%	52.39	-88.05	23.61	0.76	1.25
Alan Swinbank	17	64	26.56%	66.59	19.95	42.19	2.24	2.01
Jonjo O'Neill	11	50	22.00%	64.34	-13.48	28.00	1.74	1.78
Venetia Williams	10	33	30.30%	54.40	13.53	33.33	2.43	1.90
Charlie Longsdon	10	35	28.57%	73.44	-12.2	44.29	2.17	2.82
James Moffatt	8	44	18.18%	53.79	-9.84	30.11	1.48	1.16
John Wade	8	54	14.81%	49.18	13.44	20.94	1.26	0.95

CARTMEL

Trainer	Wins	Runs	Strike Rate	% Rivals Beaten	P/L	Run To Form %	Impact Value	Market Value
Donald McCain	28	105	26.67%	63.31	-5.19	33.33	1.81	1.85
Dianne Sayer	12	94	12.77%	54.38	-12.67	22.80	1.07	1.13
James Moffatt	10	83	12.05%	52.12	27.25	20.74	0.99	0.94
Harriet Graham	9	36	25.00%	47.77	0.24	32.26	1.78	1.14
Peter Bowen	7	31	22.58%	66.73	-1.38	33.06	1.85	1.79
Nigel Twiston-Davies	6	31	19.35%	60.25	-9.5	24.19	1.37	1.68
Jonjo O'Neill	6	18	33.33%	67.30	4.8	38.89	2.44	2.12
John Quinn	6	16	37.50%	80.64	7.25	52.50	2.71	2.42
Brian Ellison	5	26	19.23%	64.65	10	34.62	1.38	1.80
Alistair Whillans	5	28	17.86%	58.38	15.5	32.00	1.61	1.20

CATTERICK BRIDGE

Trainer	Wins	Runs	Strike Rate	% Rivals Beaten	P/L	Run To Form %	Impact Value	Market Value
Donald McCain	39	168	23.21%	58.49	-7.77	36.77	1.78	1.75
Sue Smith	19	101	18.81%	59.76	36.79	33.22	1.60	1.37
Keith Reveley	16	73	21.92%	60.27	-5.78	32.88	2.02	1.84
Brian Ellison	15	67	22.39%	65.30	-19.11	39.29	1.79	1.96
John Ferguson	13	21	61.90%	80.61	16	72.22	5.21	3.64
Micky Hammond	9	138	6.52%	50.61	-86.5	17.47	0.59	0.89
Jonjo O'Neill	8	29	27.59%	57.81	3.16	42.24	1.84	1.68
John Wade	8	58	13.79%	52.26	-18.21	31.27	1.25	1.02
Malcolm Jefferson	7	38	18.42%	58.37	7	32.24	1.60	1.15
David O'Meara	5	18	27.78%	69.43	20.5	37.04	2.68	1.70

CHELTENHAM

Trainer	Wins	Runs	Strike Rate	% Rivals Beaten	P/L	Run To Form %	Impact Value	Market Value
Paul Nicholls	59	441	13.38%	55.57	-9.59	30.82	1.35	1.65
Nicky Henderson	47	384	12.24%	56.55	-88.96	26.84	1.47	1.68
Philip Hobbs	38	274	13.87%	56.91	-30.18	29.60	1.63	1.54
David Pipe	31	287	10.80%	51.04	-22.72	20.93	1.36	1.54
W. P. Mullins, Ireland	31	257	12.06%	57.16	-80.46	30.42	1.71	1.97
Nigel Twiston-Davies	26	263	9.89%	51.28	-102.4	25.45	1.04	1.18
Jonjo O'Neill	23	192	11.98%	50.75	19.96	23.44	1.54	1.43
Alan King	17	183	9.29%	54.98	-27.54	30.17	1.12	1.34
Martin Keighley	12	95	12.63%	54.01	4.88	26.32	1.43	1.15
Fergal O'Brien	11	86	12.79%	53.56	41	31.40	1.57	0.98

CHEPSTOW

Trainer	Wins	Runs	Strike Rate	% Rivals Beaten	P/L	Run To Form %	Impact Value	Market Value
Philip Hobbs	28	146	19.18%	65.29	-23.87	34.34	1.88	1.93
David Pipe	24	120	20.00%	59.35	7.62	30.53	2.04	1.78
Paul Nicholls	23	151	15.23%	60.04	-88.29	26.34	1.40	2.55
Evan Williams	23	169	13.61%	54.18	11.91	23.00	1.17	1.20
Rebecca Curtis	19	120	15.83%	59.04	-36.91	29.38	1.36	1.80
Peter Bowen	19	101	18.81%	54.14	30.73	30.56	1.85	1.21
Nigel Twiston-Davies	16	112	14.29%	55.78	-11.73	26.28	1.43	1.34
Venetia Williams	15	132	11.36%	54.56	-42.68	23.62	1.02	1.29
Jonjo O'Neill	13	113	11.50%	51.72	-46.46	20.14	1.20	1.50
Alan King	11	66	16.67%	60.72	-20.98	30.30	1.60	1.62

DONCASTER

Trainer	Wins	Runs	Strike Rate	% Rivals Beaten	P/L	Run To Form %	Impact Value	Market Value
Nicky Henderson	39	102	38.24%	72.39	42.34	61.76	3.02	2.75
Keith Reveley	20	132	15.15%	57.83	-1.45	32.78	1.36	1.15
Alan King	19	100	19.00%	59.63	-9.31	34.75	1.60	1.85
Paul Nicholls	16	66	24.24%	57.74	-20.78	37.88	1.66	2.04
John Ferguson	11	40	27.50%	66.73	1.73	43.10	2.25	2.99
John Quinn	10	29	34.48%	67.01	40.25	46.93	2.85	1.58
Emma Lavelle	9	33	27.27%	58.12	7.33	33.33	2.64	1.91
Harry Fry	9	25	36.00%	59.55	4.54	52.00	2.46	1.89
James Ewart	8	38	21.05%	60.94	6.5	35.26	1.55	1.18
Kim Bailey	8	48	16.67%	54.31	1.6	30.02	1.49	1.61

EXETER

Trainer	Wins	Runs	Strike Rate	% Rivals Beaten	P/L	Run To Form %	Impact Value	Market Value
Philip Hobbs	44	224	19.64%	59.96	-46.5	35.80	1.66	1.95
Paul Nicholls	35	134	26.12%	66.57	-27.36	39.30	1.94	3.00
David Pipe	31	196	15.82%	56.30	-51.86	28.29	1.37	1.63
Colin Tizzard	22	148	14.86%	59.54	-42.79	27.37	1.27	1.31
Venetia Williams	17	92	18.48%	53.36	11.71	26.35	1.53	1.25
Harry Fry	17	43	39.53%	80.83	38.47	63.28	3.63	2.59
Alan King	16	79	20.25%	59.59	-7.73	33.94	1.75	1.51
Victor Dartnall	16	102	15.69%	54.14	5.25	27.25	1.38	1.30
Susan Gardner	16	123	13.01%	48.73	8.33	20.52	1.21	0.91
Emma Lavelle	12	85	14.12%	55.36	-37.47	23.81	1.22	1.62

FAKENHAM

Trainer	Wins	Runs	Strike Rate	% Rivals Beaten	P/L	Run To Form %	Impact Value	Market Value
Lucy Wadham	18	67	26.87%	63.92	25.04	43.79	1.81	1.60
Nicky Henderson	17	33	51.52%	79.02	0.93	57.58	3.17	2.93
Tim Vaughan	14	68	20.59%	51.47	-27.88	26.92	1.26	1.55
Peter Bowen	11	29	37.93%	69.68	12.98	51.72	2.50	1.85
John Ferguson	9	32	28.13%	63.98	4.61	40.74	2.01	2.43
Neil Mulholland	9	33	27.27%	57.53	17.02	39.39	1.81	1.22
Neil King	9	73	12.33%	48.16	-1.9	16.63	0.78	0.96
Alex Hales	8	47	17.02%	54.61	8.23	25.53	1.20	1.12
David Pipe	8	14	57.14%	79.84	10.47	64.29	2.85	2.17
Dan Skelton	8	29	27.59%	63.04	-3.84	41.38	1.60	1.95

FFOS LAS

Trainer	Wins	Runs	Strike Rate	% Rivals Beaten	P/L	Run To Form %	Impact Value	Market Value
Rebecca Curtis	53	196	27.04%	67.35	32.74	39.65	1.95	1.92
Peter Bowen	52	351	14.81%	55.27	-96.43	28.34	1.08	1.17
Evan Williams	51	374	13.64%	49.89	-24.31	20.11	0.95	1.10
Nigel Twiston-Davies	33	169	19.53%	54.53	1.99	29.64	1.33	1.38
Jonjo O'Neill	32	138	23.19%	58.94	21.15	36.24	1.75	1.75
Tim Vaughan	27	245	11.02%	50.43	-118.04	19.65	0.79	1.18
David Pipe	21	132	15.91%	56.73	-30.28	26.99	1.24	1.74
Nicky Henderson	15	35	42.86%	73.55	-0.31	54.29	3.33	3.06
Bernard Llewellyn	15	126	11.90%	46.07	50.64	21.94	0.86	0.80
Debra Hamer	12	70	17.14%	41.87	7.46	23.07	1.34	0.88

FONTWELL PARK

Trainer	Wins	Runs	Strike Rate	% Rivals Beaten	P/L	Run To Form %	Impact Value	Market Value
Chris Gordon	42	297	14.14%	51.25	-28.41	25.31	1.09	1.02
Gary Moore	40	293	13.65%	51.92	-20.75	23.52	1.09	1.28
Paul Nicholls	26	69	37.68%	69.92	-4.69	47.16	2.18	2.21
Neil Mulholland	23	114	20.18%	52.21	11.27	27.14	1.50	1.22
Anthony Honeyball	19	60	31.67%	70.83	15.63	44.61	2.43	2.26
Charlie Longsdon	19	96	19.79%	62.98	-26.47	37.75	1.65	1.89
Tim Vaughan	16	109	14.68%	50.05	-33.54	20.94	1.06	1.53
David Pipe	15	72	20.83%	61.67	-14.73	24.10	1.76	1.97
Oliver Sherwood	15	68	22.06%	63.09	4.14	40.01	1.63	1.64
Lawney Hill	15	67	22.39%	56.89	1.83	32.92	1.70	1.26

HAYDOCK

Trainer	Wins	Runs	Strike Rate	% Rivals Beaten	P/L	Run To Form %	Impact Value	Market Value
Donald McCain	28	139	20.14%	53.68	-13.4	32.43	1.55	1.44
Paul Nicholls	16	68	23.53%	65.26	-2.83	35.89	1.62	1.78
Sue Smith	14	122	11.48%	56.22	35.45	27.25	0.92	1.12
Venetia Williams	14	99	14.14%	47.13	-19.8	20.20	1.27	1.23
David Pipe	13	80	16.25%	58.92	35.21	29.11	1.79	1.43
Nigel Twiston-Davies	10	85	11.76%	53.68	-41.55	27.00	1.04	1.25
Nicky Henderson	10	57	17.54%	55.96	-23.49	25.73	1.30	1.98
Lucinda Russell	10	75	13.33%	43.41	6.33	17.33	1.10	0.91
Brian Ellison	9	63	14.29%	59.09	2.75	29.63	1.50	1.17
Alan King	9	53	16.98%	58.14	-10.06	30.90	1.56	1.27

HEXHAM

Trainer	Wins	Runs	Strike Rate	% Rivals Beaten	P/L	Run To Form %	Impact Value	Market Value
Lucinda Russell	49	240	20.42%	57.75	20.86	29.61	1.59	1.50
Sue Smith	21	130	16.15%	59.92	-35.46	30.65	1.33	1.39
Donald McCain	16	115	13.91%	53.31	-74.4	19.94	1.03	1.99
Brian Ellison	13	58	22.41%	62.22	10.61	31.50	1.67	1.77
Ferdy Murphy, France	12	73	16.44%	51.51	18.5	23.97	1.29	1.09
N. W. Alexander	12	73	16.44%	52.55	9.65	22.20	1.36	1.22
Stuart Coltherd	11	48	22.92%	57.60	64	33.13	1.87	1.19
Martin Todhunter	11	82	13.41%	46.10	4.38	17.07	1.12	1.01
Nicky Richards	10	30	33.33%	58.92	22.04	40.00	2.71	1.48
Micky Hammond	10	69	14.49%	49.45	-34.72	19.66	1.20	1.40

HUNTINGDON

Trainer	Wins	Runs	Strike Rate	% Rivals Beaten	P/L	Run To Form %	Impact Value	Market Value
Nicky Henderson	30	83	36.14%	73.99	-0.8	48.13	3.01	3.14
Jonjo O'Neill	27	114	23.68%	56.21	3.37	28.58	2.10	1.66
Alan King	26	113	23.01%	62.53	6.28	37.42	1.95	2.08
John Ferguson	23	63	36.51%	77.63	25.05	49.13	3.05	2.99
Charlie Longsdon	17	105	16.19%	54.13	-24.65	29.98	1.26	1.57
Kim Bailey	17	62	27.42%	62.07	51	45.52	2.32	1.25
Venetia Williams	14	77	18.18%	59.74	-4.59	31.53	1.44	1.46
Gary Moore	13	88	14.77%	50.90	13.46	25.15	1.19	1.23
Neil King	11	108	10.19%	50.58	19.75	25.30	0.78	0.90
Dan Skelton	9	66	13.64%	57.20	-34.13	32.03	1.01	1.53

TRAINERS FOR COURSES

KELSO

Trainer	Wins	Runs	Strike Rate	% Rivals Beaten	P/L	Run To Form %	Impact Value	Market Value
Donald McCain	38	160	23.75%	58.00	33.37	32.53	1.83	1.99
Lucinda Russell	33	285	11.58%	53.69	-107.51	21.77	0.95	1.28
Nicky Richards	26	117	22.22%	59.08	17.13	30.08	1.95	1.69
N. W. Alexander	22	170	12.94%	48.85	7.7	23.67	1.12	1.06
James Ewart	15	101	14.85%	52.16	-10.71	24.69	1.25	1.37
Rose Dobbin	13	119	10.92%	54.35	0.5	20.50	0.99	1.07
Stuart Coltherd	12	94	12.77%	43.91	46.63	18.44	1.08	0.83
Chris Grant	11	83	13.25%	52.03	94.88	25.63	1.15	1.03
Malcolm Jefferson	10	61	16.39%	62.37	-11.7	24.29	1.38	1.61
Dianne Sayer	9	110	8.18%	53.85	-44	19.47	0.71	0.98

KEMPTON PARK

Trainer	Wins	Runs	Strike Rate	% Rivals Beaten	P/L	Run To Form %	Impact Value	Market Value
Nicky Henderson	74	240	30.83%	66.64	83.26	42.02	2.54	2.38
Paul Nicholls	35	187	18.72%	60.04	-36.19	35.41	1.46	1.90
Alan King	22	187	11.76%	55.79	-90.76	26.97	1.04	1.58
Philip Hobbs	14	116	12.07%	57.09	-56.84	24.79	1.05	1.59
Emma Lavelle	14	75	18.67%	55.48	2.27	34.24	1.65	1.61
Jonjo O'Neill	13	103	12.62%	49.44	-36.8	21.88	1.27	1.30
Tom George	12	60	20.00%	56.75	10.5	36.67	1.72	1.24
Harry Fry	12	48	25.00%	64.63	49.32	35.33	2.44	2.04
Charlie Longsdon	10	75	13.33%	50.28	-7.33	26.67	1.21	1.38
Colin Tizzard	9	71	12.68%	56.78	-29.03	28.41	1.03	1.18

LEICESTER

Trainer	Wins	Runs	Strike Rate	% Rivals Beaten	P/L	Run To Form %	Impact Value	Market Value
Nigel Twiston-Davies	19	84	22.62%	58.52	26.28	32.86	1.67	1.45
Tom George	14	53	26.42%	62.49	12.35	46.10	1.98	1.60
David Pipe	13	33	39.39%	68.63	10.72	46.69	2.88	2.24
Venetia Williams	13	49	26.53%	60.75	-6.63	32.18	1.85	1.62
Tony Carroll	8	75	10.67%	44.27	-13	14.85	0.80	0.84
Caroline Bailey	8	48	16.67%	49.83	-12.29	25.67	1.20	0.93
Nicky Henderson	7	25	28.00%	65.08	3.55	36.00	1.91	2.17
Ian Williams	6	20	30.00%	63.36	-1.97	42.08	2.44	1.40
Fergal O'Brien	6	33	18.18%	55.59	17.13	40.58	1.24	1.32
John Ferguson	5	9	55.56%	83.91	1.07	66.67	4.42	3.60

LINGFIELD PARK

Trainer	Wins	Runs	Strike Rate	% Rivals Beaten	P/L	Run To Form %	Impact Value	Market Value
Gary Moore	11	86	12.79%	52.50	-22.33	25.69	0.94	1.35
Warren Greatrex	10	22	45.45%	70.81	26.99	45.45	3.56	2.34
Seamus Mullins	9	47	19.15%	50.99	69.5	21.88	1.36	0.91
David Pipe	6	22	27.27%	67.33	-2.53	37.73	2.50	2.49
Venetia Williams	6	49	12.24%	54.69	12.63	26.53	0.87	1.37
Nicky Henderson	6	25	24.00%	65.76	-2.93	50.00	1.77	3.08
Tim Vaughan	5	22	22.73%	54.61	-1.59	22.73	1.70	1.86
Paul Webber	5	16	31.25%	74.04	34.75	31.25	2.88	1.73
Dan Skelton	5	9	55.56%	79.63	16	64.44	3.25	1.53
Nigel Twiston-Davies	5	26	19.23%	62.51	2.08	34.62	1.29	1.43

LUDLOW

Trainer	Wins	Runs	Strike Rate	% Rivals Beaten	P/L	Run To Form %	Impact Value	Market Value
Evan Williams	52	290	17.93%	54.69	-48.08	28.12	1.40	1.44
Nicky Henderson	29	103	28.16%	67.51	-40.8	39.47	2.43	2.99
Philip Hobbs	24	110	21.82%	62.20	-15.52	33.26	1.96	2.20
Nigel Twiston-Davies	18	154	11.69%	56.62	-63.02	25.52	1.02	1.32
Henry Daly	18	124	14.52%	61.51	-39.9	29.53	1.24	1.37
Venetia Williams	17	143	11.89%	54.52	-59.8	20.23	1.05	1.38
Tom George	15	63	23.81%	63.37	-4.06	36.20	1.97	1.50
David Pipe	10	55	18.18%	59.52	5.91	26.01	1.53	1.40
Dan Skelton	10	49	20.41%	59.74	4.8	32.74	1.86	1.63
Ian Williams	10	57	17.54%	56.09	-7.18	30.12	1.56	1.27

MARKET RASEN

Trainer	Wins	Runs	Strike Rate	% Rivals Beaten	P/L	Run To Form %	Impact Value	Market Value
Charlie Longsdon	33	132	25.00%	61.43	-20.34	39.15	1.97	1.90
Jonjo O'Neill	32	223	14.35%	52.38	-69.63	25.85	1.12	1.55
Brian Ellison	25	143	17.48%	53.26	15.69	29.22	1.43	1.30
Peter Bowen	22	98	22.45%	59.02	1.29	32.99	1.95	1.63
Nicky Henderson	22	69	31.88%	67.04	19.13	38.93	2.64	2.42
Malcolm Jefferson	17	100	17.00%	56.92	9.88	30.61	1.35	1.25
John Ferguson	17	58	29.31%	71.16	4.67	43.27	2.47	2.62
Donald McCain	14	105	13.33%	49.13	-10.78	21.49	0.95	1.48
Dr Richard Newland	14	56	25.00%	62.34	21.23	34.48	2.14	1.99
Chris Bealby	13	87	14.94%	47.72	-24.47	26.96	1.18	1.05

TRAINERS FOR COURSES

MUSSELBURGH

Trainer	Wins	Runs	Strike Rate	% Rivals Beaten	P/L	Run To Form %	Impact Value	Market Value
Donald McCain	33	143	23.08%	59.18	19.74	35.19	1.68	1.70
Lucinda Russell	27	249	10.84%	52.22	-88.05	21.41	0.87	1.17
Brian Ellison	13	122	10.66%	54.69	-60.37	23.18	0.89	1.34
James Ewart	13	92	14.13%	53.53	-27.31	31.83	1.17	1.44
John Ferguson	11	38	28.95%	67.57	0.79	35.96	2.28	2.43
Jim Goldie	11	115	9.57%	44.11	-39.59	16.97	0.84	0.91
Sandy Thomson	9	42	21.43%	60.19	38.5	41.49	1.86	1.28
Peter Niven	9	32	28.13%	60.46	39.25	33.09	2.85	1.39
Chris Grant	9	89	10.11%	49.79	-28.75	19.98	0.85	0.88
Nicky Richards	9	48	18.75%	56.71	2.03	20.83	1.85	1.96

NEWBURY

Trainer	Wins	Runs	Strike Rate	% Rivals Beaten	P/L	Run To Form %	Impact Value	Market Value
Nicky Henderson	39	199	19.60%	58.58	-58.38	31.90	1.79	2.14
Paul Nicholls	38	196	19.39%	60.99	-17.83	35.59	1.56	1.93
Philip Hobbs	24	139	17.27%	59.46	76.93	30.81	1.68	1.64
David Pipe	22	138	15.94%	54.22	-5.41	24.40	1.54	1.32
Alan King	22	189	11.64%	61.39	-70.8	30.81	1.07	1.50
Nigel Twiston-Davies	14	107	13.08%	49.23	15.74	27.10	1.21	1.06
Venetia Williams	13	105	12.38%	52.89	-47.53	28.18	1.05	1.29
Harry Fry	12	42	28.57%	69.36	0.92	48.73	2.31	2.20
Jonjo O'Neill	11	100	11.00%	49.89	-35.39	23.43	1.11	1.32
Warren Greatrex	10	58	17.24%	55.60	-10.25	27.59	1.57	1.17

NEWCASTLE

Trainer	Wins	Runs	Strike Rate	% Rivals Beaten	P/L	Run To Form %	Impact Value	Market Value
Lucinda Russell	25	179	13.97%	54.35	-26.63	25.04	1.06	1.32
Donald McCain	21	106	19.81%	59.86	7.65	33.14	1.45	1.84
N. W. Alexander	18	111	16.22%	49.58	-13.68	28.67	1.35	1.12
Keith Reveley	18	98	18.37%	61.70	-25.7	33.50	1.45	1.66
Sue Smith	16	117	13.68%	53.97	-29.34	26.73	1.12	1.36
Nicky Richards	15	60	25.00%	60.04	6.42	33.00	2.24	2.01
Chris Grant	10	128	7.81%	46.51	-73.54	18.26	0.66	0.92
John Wade	9	67	13.43%	49.95	-34.84	24.94	1.15	1.10
Malcolm Jefferson	9	46	19.57%	64.10	1.75	36.23	1.73	1.61
Ann Hamilton	8	32	25.00%	59.98	4.82	43.75	1.56	1.25

NEWTON ABBOT

Trainer	Wins	Runs	Strike Rate	% Rivals Beaten	P/L	Run To Form %	Impact Value	Market Value
Paul Nicholls	40	132	30.30%	68.69	-12.38	45.97	2.03	2.25
Philip Hobbs	30	159	18.87%	61.93	-1	33.95	1.52	1.68
Jonjo O'Neill	25	118	21.19%	51.78	-5.02	27.81	1.86	1.75
Evan Williams	24	130	18.46%	57.29	-35.98	28.68	1.30	1.35
David Pipe	20	172	11.63%	52.41	-78.07	23.35	1.08	1.52
Tim Vaughan	19	129	14.73%	52.90	-46.18	25.10	1.20	1.52
Martin Hill	14	92	15.22%	52.07	10.38	25.44	1.29	1.14
Colin Tizzard	14	129	10.85%	52.63	-41.25	23.81	0.84	1.27
John Ferguson	14	37	37.84%	69.42	10.17	53.30	2.88	2.38
Peter Bowen	12	90	13.33%	59.51	-13.96	24.19	1.14	1.61

PERTH

Trainer	Wins	Runs	Strike Rate	% Rivals Beaten	P/L	Run To Form %	Impact Value	Market Value
Gordon Elliott, Ireland	77	261	29.50%	63.64	14.54	43.41	1.99	2.13
Lucinda Russell	43	436	9.86%	49.67	-131.17	24.14	0.72	1.06
Nigel Twiston-Davies	22	108	20.37%	59.96	1.35	32.45	1.69	1.82
Donald McCain	22	129	17.05%	55.46	-32.26	28.88	1.12	1.55
Tim Vaughan	18	55	32.73%	68.94	21.61	44.39	1.93	1.58
Peter Bowen	16	41	39.02%	70.93	20.63	48.78	2.79	2.05
Lisa Harrison	16	113	14.16%	55.71	-9.17	29.85	1.14	1.00
Nicky Richards	14	88	15.91%	57.06	-4.92	31.43	1.31	1.22
Jim Goldie	13	101	12.87%	49.25	-7.63	19.13	0.99	1.07
N. W. Alexander	13	145	8.97%	45.36	11.5	17.68	0.76	0.84

PLUMPTON

Trainer	Wins	Runs	Strike Rate	% Rivals Beaten	P/L	Run To Form %	Impact Value	Market Value
Gary Moore	42	225	18.67%	60.03	-40.24	30.39	1.40	1.55
Alan King	23	57	40.35%	72.47	1.3	49.42	2.84	2.56
Chris Gordon	19	151	12.58%	52.07	26.66	21.15	1.00	1.20
Venetia Williams	17	64	26.56%	58.21	-9.35	30.40	1.98	1.90
Seamus Mullins	17	153	11.11%	49.14	-58.17	20.67	0.78	1.02
Suzy Smith	16	68	23.53%	63.52	75.88	35.72	2.03	1.23
David Pipe	16	58	27.59%	66.31	7.35	39.63	2.02	2.24
David Bridgwater	15	63	23.81%	63.14	0.41	34.40	1.70	1.45
Paul Henderson	13	65	20.00%	49.56	19.88	27.02	1.45	0.99
Charlie Longsdon	13	62	20.97%	56.15	-18.07	32.79	1.69	1.85

TRAINERS FOR COURSES

SANDOWN PARK

Trainer	Wins	Runs	Strike Rate	% Rivals Beaten	P/L	Run To Form %	Impact Value	Market Value
Nicky Henderson	37	155	23.87%	60.16	28.49	35.11	2.01	1.84
Paul Nicholls	36	187	19.25%	61.49	-12.86	34.37	1.44	1.77
Gary Moore	24	111	21.62%	46.66	95.15	28.83	1.72	0.97
Philip Hobbs	15	93	16.13%	59.07	-15.1	34.97	1.46	1.57
Venetia Williams	13	113	11.50%	50.78	-52.43	24.78	0.98	1.20
Alan King	10	72	13.89%	54.65	-10.17	29.17	1.29	1.38
David Pipe	8	79	10.13%	49.51	-38.85	20.70	1.15	1.46
Jonjo O'Neill	7	75	9.33%	51.10	-30.38	17.89	0.89	1.40
Emma Lavelle	6	29	20.69%	62.51	8	31.99	1.83	1.44
Charlie Longsdon	6	51	11.76%	52.04	-2.75	21.57	1.18	1.23

SEDGEFIELD

Trainer	Wins	Runs	Strike Rate	% Rivals Beaten	P/L	Run To Form %	Impact Value	Market Value
Donald McCain	65	248	26.21%	59.88	-31.54	34.92	1.78	1.99
Sue Smith	32	221	14.48%	57.81	-37	32.22	1.10	1.34
Malcolm Jefferson	30	103	29.13%	65.24	54.29	37.52	2.14	1.43
Micky Hammond	25	145	17.24%	53.87	-3.35	25.43	1.28	1.05
Brian Ellison	25	120	20.83%	59.24	-27.35	28.82	1.52	1.74
Chris Grant	18	136	13.24%	48.82	-11.94	22.93	0.98	0.86
Kenneth Slack	14	30	46.67%	76.08	33.92	53.57	3.53	1.89
Dianne Sayer	14	87	16.09%	50.65	-14.75	22.99	1.27	1.09
Keith Reveley	14	58	24.14%	60.44	29.04	38.55	1.92	1.54
Barry Murtagh	10	79	12.66%	50.75	10.83	17.72	1.04	0.93

SOUTHWELL

Trainer	Wins	Runs	Strike Rate	% Rivals Beaten	P/L	Run To Form %	Impact Value	Market Value
Jonjo O'Neill	32	171	18.71%	61.42	-29.44	30.31	1.62	1.84
Charlie Longsdon	23	83	27.71%	61.60	8.09	36.76	2.17	2.02
Caroline Bailey	18	75	24.00%	56.84	46.96	32.27	1.76	1.15
Tom George	17	57	29.82%	68.44	25.88	50.37	2.48	1.75
Peter Bowen	13	65	20.00%	58.29	13.33	26.65	1.65	1.66
Nicky Henderson	13	54	24.07%	71.80	-20.83	38.07	1.89	2.83
Keith Reveley	13	62	20.97%	60.91	4.63	36.08	1.72	1.58
Kim Bailey	12	41	29.27%	66.66	27.73	47.28	2.10	1.55
Dan Skelton	12	50	24.00%	64.67	7	43.00	1.86	1.90
Tim Vaughan	12	89	13.48%	56.89	-17.85	20.51	1.00	1.46

STRATFORD

Trainer	Wins	Runs	Strike Rate	% Rivals Beaten	P/L	Run To Form %	Impact Value	Market Value
Jonjo O'Neill	24	116	20.69%	52.93	24.44	27.19	1.74	1.42
John Ferguson	19	48	39.58%	73.91	4.88	50.36	3.34	2.85
Tim Vaughan	18	115	15.65%	55.77	-8.92	25.99	1.34	1.30
Philip Hobbs	17	77	22.08%	59.32	12.82	30.88	1.78	1.54
Warren Greatrex	16	48	33.33%	71.58	21.2	41.67	2.61	2.14
Nigel Twiston-Davies	14	102	13.73%	58.01	-12.13	24.76	1.24	1.53
Charlie Longsdon	14	66	21.21%	55.41	13.23	26.57	1.89	1.86
Evan Williams	13	86	15.12%	52.36	-26.5	20.71	1.22	1.37
David Pipe	12	68	17.65%	57.54	-6.96	28.82	1.45	1.70
Dan Skelton	11	53	20.75%	61.38	-7.48	35.08	1.60	1.61

TAUNTON

Trainer	Wins	Runs	Strike Rate	% Rivals Beaten	P/L	Run To Form %	Impact Value	Market Value
Paul Nicholls	53	177	29.94%	74.72	-6.06	48.99	2.38	2.69
David Pipe	28	196	14.29%	52.12	-68.3	26.60	1.30	1.41
Philip Hobbs	24	146	16.44%	62.87	-55.76	27.40	1.57	2.00
Evan Williams	18	112	16.07%	45.20	14.58	20.54	1.29	1.17
Venetia Williams	17	83	20.48%	59.49	5.65	25.28	1.65	1.60
Colin Tizzard	16	120	13.33%	55.15	-32	24.73	1.14	1.25
Harry Fry	12	55	21.82%	74.15	-14.63	48.42	2.17	2.65
Nicky Henderson	11	41	26.83%	61.70	-2.26	41.71	2.35	2.71
Anthony Honeyball	10	59	16.95%	53.74	23.71	27.37	1.53	1.19
Jeremy Scott	10	64	15.63%	61.24	0.25	31.12	1.56	1.29

TOWCESTER

Trainer	Wins	Runs	Strike Rate	% Rivals Beaten	P/L	Run To Form %	Impact Value	Market Value
Kim Bailey	18	71	25.35%	60.02	15.85	30.46	2.24	1.91
Alan King	16	50	32.00%	74.26	11	43.22	2.79	2.58
Nicky Henderson	15	54	27.78%	72.77	-5.73	35.30	2.59	3.32
Venetia Williams	15	77	19.48%	61.92	-29.93	25.04	1.46	1.66
Fergal O'Brien	15	78	19.23%	58.83	-3.45	28.83	1.71	1.63
David Pipe	14	57	24.56%	58.26	0.59	33.33	2.15	2.45
Charlie Longsdon	12	67	17.91%	60.05	19.98	27.49	1.48	1.33
Jonjo O'Neill	12	98	12.24%	54.30	-49.84	25.22	1.16	1.56
Martin Keighley	11	68	16.18%	55.27	-13.5	23.91	1.40	1.25
Oliver Sherwood	11	56	19.64%	62.81	-5.16	36.50	1.50	1.64

TRAINERS FOR COURSES

UTTOXETER

Trainer	Wins	Runs	Strike Rate	% Rivals Beaten	P/L	Run To Form %	Impact Value	Market Value
Jonjo O'Neill	37	258	14.34%	52.35	-67.04	26.01	1.28	1.77
Nigel Twiston-Davies	25	124	20.16%	58.83	16.84	30.44	1.81	1.48
David Pipe	25	140	17.86%	60.72	-5.07	25.22	1.64	1.91
Donald McCain	25	219	11.42%	51.64	-91.18	22.03	0.93	1.55
Charlie Longsdon	23	103	22.33%	61.22	-27.02	38.61	1.95	2.14
Tim Vaughan	21	160	13.13%	54.21	-47.93	21.71	1.06	1.45
Neil King	21	103	20.39%	60.58	11.87	30.98	1.69	1.30
Dr Richard Newland	18	57	31.58%	68.43	14.41	40.72	2.63	2.22
Peter Bowen	17	113	15.04%	54.25	-38.62	25.43	1.32	1.48
Philip Hobbs	16	82	19.51%	60.59	4.58	28.50	1.74	1.74

WARWICK

Trainer	Wins	Runs	Strike Rate	% Rivals Beaten	P/L	Run To Form %	Impact Value	Market Value
Alan King	22	112	19.64%	67.01	-48.68	34.95	1.74	2.10
Philip Hobbs	21	88	23.86%	61.28	-1.99	35.61	2.17	1.97
Nigel Twiston-Davies	17	136	12.50%	52.88	-65.23	24.00	1.05	1.31
Jonjo O'Neill	17	120	14.17%	52.70	9.99	23.77	1.44	1.34
Venetia Williams	15	100	15.00%	57.07	-21.7	25.68	1.21	1.35
Dan Skelton	14	66	21.21%	59.10	-13.76	32.78	1.76	1.82
Paul Nicholls	13	40	32.50%	69.35	8.13	49.71	2.14	2.09
Charlie Longsdon	12	90	13.33%	57.13	-7.36	27.11	1.17	1.60
Nicky Henderson	11	46	23.91%	63.73	-16.93	31.61	1.99	2.49
Henry Daly	9	67	13.43%	52.93	-0.25	22.39	1.36	1.29

WETHERBY

Trainer	Wins	Runs	Strike Rate	% Rivals Beaten	P/L	Run To Form %	Impact Value	Market Value
Sue Smith	30	227	13.22%	52.73	-88.35	26.66	1.11	1.30
Donald McCain	23	151	15.23%	49.78	-43.99	26.21	1.21	1.53
Brian Ellison	19	118	16.10%	58.19	-9.5	27.04	1.43	1.58
Jonjo O'Neill	18	78	23.08%	65.31	-11.06	37.61	1.83	2.02
Malcolm Jefferson	15	83	18.07%	55.98	42.18	28.66	1.53	1.38
Warren Greatrex	14	38	36.84%	70.14	24.34	44.61	2.91	2.64
Micky Hammond	14	188	7.45%	45.54	-90.92	15.74	0.66	0.93
Lucinda Russell	13	123	10.57%	49.59	-30.63	22.47	0.85	1.26
Philip Kirby	12	88	13.64%	48.01	-24.07	19.17	1.31	1.13
Charlie Longsdon	12	47	25.53%	59.49	1.21	34.04	2.42	2.14

WINCANTON

Trainer	Wins	Runs	Strike Rate	% Rivals Beaten	P/L	Run To Form %	Impact Value	Market Value
Paul Nicholls	79	260	30.38%	67.73	-7.73	44.22	2.32	2.52
Colin Tizzard	33	215	15.35%	53.96	-8.17	25.96	1.34	1.33
David Pipe	32	177	18.08%	55.77	-11.48	30.79	1.69	1.77
Philip Hobbs	27	166	16.27%	56.26	-26.04	26.96	1.39	1.70
Harry Fry	17	71	23.94%	67.94	5.5	43.30	2.17	2.10
Jeremy Scott	16	115	13.91%	54.61	-1.88	22.63	1.12	1.09
Venetia Williams	15	113	13.27%	59.14	-32.65	34.38	1.02	1.38
Tom George	14	66	21.21%	64.86	-11.97	31.76	1.65	1.42
Emma Lavelle	13	68	19.12%	64.56	31.25	31.21	1.71	1.53
Alan King	11	97	11.34%	61.69	-32.88	26.36	0.98	1.72

WORCESTER

Trainer	Wins	Runs	Strike Rate	% Rivals Beaten	P/L	Run To Form %	Impact Value	Market Value
Jonjo O'Neill	50	266	18.80%	56.97	-40.08	27.97	1.61	1.77
David Pipe	25	161	15.53%	55.34	-63.56	20.30	1.30	1.71
Paul Nicholls	22	68	32.35%	74.23	-5.02	45.59	2.33	2.49
Tim Vaughan	19	143	13.29%	57.91	-31.83	28.99	1.12	1.48
Peter Bowen	18	96	18.75%	54.76	-0.42	30.88	1.69	1.68
Nigel Twiston-Davies	18	111	16.22%	53.64	-11.09	24.55	1.45	1.38
Philip Hobbs	17	88	19.32%	62.65	-6.28	25.31	1.61	1.76
Donald McCain	16	107	14.95%	57.57	-10.1	26.46	1.12	1.44
John Ferguson	16	43	37.21%	67.34	-8.2	43.29	2.74	2.75
Charlie Longsdon	16	93	17.20%	61.48	-25.74	29.89	1.49	1.96

SAVE £135 A YEAR!

Race Passes are the ultimate form guide, featuring ratings, all the Timeform Flags, In-Play Hints and symbols, live Betfair prices – plus unlimited use of a 12-year archive and Horse Searches. Subscriptions give you open access to Timeform data, starting from just £10 for 24 hours, to £75 for 28 days.

Why not sign-up by Direct Debit. You'll save £5 every month and get 29 free days per year. That's worth £135.

Race Passes

Ratings. Flags. Form. In-Play.
Search any horse, any race, any time.

Find out more at timeform.com and view Race Passes on the App

Index To Photographers

INDEX